GW00566795

FORGED FROM THE DOCKS

JAMES SARFAS

First Printed in Great Britain by
Obex Publishing Ltd in 2021

Copyright James Sarfas, 2021

Hardback ISBN: 978-1-913454-56-2
Paperback ISBN: 978-1-913454-57-9
eBook ISBN: 978-1-913454-58-6

A CIP catalogue record for this book is available from
the British Library

Obex Publishing Limited
Reg. No. 121699

CONTENTS

CHAPTER 1: INTRODUCTION 4

CHAPTER 2: BORN OUT OF THE DOCKS 15

CHAPTER 3: THE WORLD AT WAR 32

CHAPTER 4: TIME APART 48

CHAPTER 5: THE DAWN OF HOOLIGANISM 56

CHAPTER 6: TENSIONS COME TO A HEAD 70

CHAPTER 7: ALL CHANGE IN THE 1990S 86

CHAPTER 8: STEPPING INTO THE 21ST CENTURY .. 103

RESULTS 140

REFERENCES 152

Chapter 1:
Introduction

Celtic v Rangers in Scotland, Boca Juniors v River Plate in Argentina and Fenerbahçe v Galatasaray in Turkey. All of these rivalries stir up a certain sort of emotion, certainly not for the faint of heart. Millwall v West Ham United is no different. A rivalry born out of the docks of Victorian-era London, the discontent and, at times, the pure hatred the clubs' two fanbases share for each other is unlike any other seen in England, so much so, that after the infamous 2009 League Cup tie between the pair, the *Sunday Times* commissioned a cartoon of two Taliban members in war-torn Afghanistan pondering if there will ever be peace between Millwall and West Ham. This game is a powder keg that has been burning away for over 120 years. The rivalry has blown the top and exploded a number of times, on occasion leading to tragedy.

The East End and south London… they're two like-for-like cultures and people.
All that separates them is the Thames.
London Evening Standard, 26 September 2003

The vibe around Millwall's original ground south of the River Thames, The Den, was sinister at best. When described to an outsider, the streets of Ilderton Road and Cold Blow Lane flanking The Den would conjure thoughts of Dickensian London, with rain-soaked streets sitting underneath a crumbling railway bridge with the intimidatory slogan of "WHU TURN BACK" crudely daubed in white paint acting as a de-facto 'no trespassers' sign. Despite its menacing and unforgiving name, Cold Blow Lane was actually named after Cold Blow Farm, which existed when New Cross was still largely agricultural. As South London rapidly became more industrialised, the farm was shut down and replaced. A series of industrial developments patchworked together, comprising of over 40 acres, now sits on this once barren pocket of the modern day London Borough of Lewisham. Despite its non-threatening history, in the mid-70s, newly appointed Millwall manager Gordon Jago proposed renaming Cold

Blow Lane to Montego Bay Avenue, which ultimately proved unsuccessful. Millwall graffiti from decades gone by is still a prominent feature on Ilderton Road and Cold Blow Lane.

Football has always been a tribal affair, with violence going hand-in-hand. Excess noise and fighting led King Edward II to outlaw the game in the capital in 1314, condemning the game as "evil". There must have been something with kings named Edward and not liking football. Edward III and Edward IV both banned the game in 1349 and 1477 respectively, with Edward IV preferring "every strong and able bodied person" to take up archery instead. The establishment has never been too keen on the idea of the game, usually played in mobs back in the day, with no fewer than eight kings of England and Scotland trying to ban the game in the medieval era. The bans never really had any real effect. Funny, that.

The rivalry between Millwall and West Ham is deeply rooted in society, a fact that other rivalries in England simply can't relate with. Millwall and West Ham, along with their fanbases, were forged out of an extremely volatile area of London. The East End has long been looked at with an air of fascination by wider British society: the Great Plague of 1665, the Jack the Ripper murders in 1888 and the sheer poverty seen in the slums before the mass clearances have all helped perpetuate a sort of mysticism surrounding the area, that has no doubt crept into outsiders' views of the two clubs. Since Millwall's move south of the River Thames in the early 20th century, the divide between the pair has strengthened, if anything.

Historically, the east and south of London have always been at odds with each other, despite the working class background that the two share. In medieval times, Southwark, south of the river, was regarded as a lawless area of the city, falling outside of the jurisdiction of the laws north of the river. In the early 1400s, brothels were banned in the City of London, forcing their owners to set up shop in Southwark. A sense of resentment developed south of the Thames towards the north side, following their turfing out. In turn, the most affluent areas of London have viewed East and South London with an air of superiority, often looking down upon their less fortunate neighbours. In more contemporary times, the Krays and the Richardson gangs both represented East and South London respectively, with the two factions feuding in the 1960s. There's no evidence to suggest the Krays and the Richardson's supported West Ham and Millwall respectively, let alone liked football at all, however, the mere existence of the two and them calling both sides of the Thames home was enough to inflame tensions between the pair. Millwall fans have often likened the two clubs with the two gangs, claiming West Ham fans, the wider population of the East End and, in turn, the Inter City Firm, have often sought stardom, whereas Millwall, along with the Richardson's, got on with life without a fuss. Although these factors may seem irrelevant in the present day, they have all helped contribute to the tribal nature between East and South London, separated by the Thames. This probably best summed up by former Inter City Firm member Cass Pennant, speaking to the *London Evening Standard* prior to a September 2003 meeting between the pair, saying "It's always been this way. You can go back to medieval times, Victorian times or the time of the Krays. The hatred has always been there", adding "to be honest it's got very little do with football and games just provide a platform for the hatred" in reference to the rivalry between the two sides of the Thames. The tribalism between East and South London still exists to the present day, with West Ham fans making light of their perceived belief that South London is more underdeveloped than their side of the river, chanting "Does the social know you're here?" and labelling Millwall's support "pikeys" at a November 2004 meeting between the two clubs. The phrases 'bandit country' and 'deep south' are still bandied about regarding Bermondsey by both sections of supporters, perhaps a hark back to days gone by. Millwall themselves have been known to chant "East London is like Bengal" in reference to the sizeable Asian population in the London Borough of Newham, where West Ham are based. In recent years, this chant has died out, however, due to the increasing intolerance of racially insensitive chants in the 21st century.

Despite the duo's differences, whether they like it or not, the two clubs share a number of similarities, no doubt enhanced by their working class origins, with many present-day fans of both clubs still belonging to the working class. West Ham and Millwall's common ground is perhaps best amplified by two of Millwall's most revered legends, Harry Cripps and Barry Kitchener, both being East London boys, beginning their careers in the youth ranks at Upton Park. The duo are now synonymous with Millwall, making a combined total of 1,049 appearances whilst at the club. Cripps and Kitchener are now woven into the very fabric of The (New) Den, with Cripps having a bar named after him at the ground and Kitchener's name now adorning the existing 5,354 capacity West Stand, renamed after the centre-back's untimely death in the spring of 2012. Just for good measure, Millwall cult hero Terry Hurlock also began his career as a youth player at West Ham.

In the 1970s, at the height of the bad blood between the two fanbases, punk band Sham 69 had a significant following from football supporters, counting on the fanbases of West Ham, Millwall and Chelsea as their main well-wishers. The incendiary nature of the genre, as well as its followers, often made for violence at Sham 69's gigs, although the violence was more of a political nature, with the fascist National Front party gaining more popularity towards the end of the decade, than to do with football allegiances. In the days of young, working class men following bands much more than the present day, there's no evidence to suggest outbreaks of violence were football related. The band's 1978 release If The Kids Are United, which reached number nine in the UK charts in July of that year, was picked up and informally adopted by West Ham and could still be heard over the tannoy at Upton Park well into the 21st century. Sham 69's 2010 release Millwall Boys is a fair bit more obvious as to what club it's referencing, especially with Millwall's rampant lion being on the cover art. Funnily enough, the members of Sham 69 never did make their footballing allegiances public. Probably a good thing in hindsight.

Another facet of social history that intrinsically links East and South London together, and therefore West Ham and Millwall, is trade unionist Jack Dash. The lifelong British Communist Party member was involved in every single dock strike between 1945 and 1970. Due to the demographics of the dockland areas, the striking dockers would've been predominantly West Ham and Millwall supporters. Born into poverty in 1907 in Southwark, a Millwall supporting area, Dash was orphaned at a young age and later moved to the other side of the river to Stepney, a fervent West Ham area.

He died in 1989, with his legacy being recognised a year later with the naming of Jack Dash House on the Isle of Dogs, an area with links to both clubs, by Tower Hamlets Council.

Additionally, despite West Ham having the likes of Chelsea and Tottenham Hotspur as their London derbies and Millwall counting Charlton Athletic and Crystal Palace as their local rivals, West Ham and Millwall have always remained each other's fiercest rivals, with the similarities between the two bonding the pair together.

Despite the club's close proximities, crossing the divide has never been too common between the two, especially since Millwall's move to South London at the beginning of the 20th century. At the time of writing, goalkeeper David Martin, son of West Ham legend Alvin Martin, is the most recent player to cross the Thames, swapping Millwall for West Ham in the summer of 2019. Moves between high-profile players are even less common; Martin made 15 appearances in all competitions for the Lions over the course of two seasons. Controversy reigned in August 2004 when West Ham signed Moses

Ashikodi, Millwall's youngest ever player, following his release from Millwall. Ashikodi's release came after the England under-17 international pulled a knife on fellow Millwall forward Mark McCammon in the club canteen following an argument after training. Following calls from the Millwall Supporters' Club to terminate his contract, Ashikodi was sacked at the age of 16. Despite West Ham manager Alan Pardew calling Ashikodi a "major talent" who was "getting a last chance with us", the Nigerian born forward left the club after two seasons, failing to make a first team appearance during his time at Upton Park. Unsurprisingly, Ashikodi has been involved in a number of controversies throughout his career. It's even rarer is that players will be loaned from one to another, with Dale Gordon and Glen Johnson being the only players to be loaned out from Upton Park to The Den, the latter player receiving a less than eloquent call of "shoot him" on a forum post on an unnamed Millwall website following his loan to the Lions. The likes of Pat Holland, Graham Paddon and Teddy Sheringham have all played for both clubs during their careers throughout the years, with various levels of indignation. A steady flow of players, including half-back Joe Blythe, who made 341 appearances for Millwall in the early 20th century, moved between the two clubs, however, transfers between Millwall and West Ham have significantly declined since the rivalry intensified during the 1970s. Former West Ham and Millwall defender Kenny Brown, son of one-time England international Ken Brown Senior, is perhaps the only man on earth who considers himself a supporter of both clubs. Brown made 79 appearances for the Hammers across five seasons, later joining Millwall, where he played 52 times, under the management of ex-Hammer Billy Bonds. Brown's admission came after re-joining Millwall in a coaching capacity in February 2016. Brown must be the only Millwall supporter born in the West Ham stronghold of Barking.

Stand closures, to help prevent one set of supporters from 'taking' the others' end, or as a general form of crowd control have been commonplace at Upton Park and The Den since the turn of the 21st century. Special measures on matchdays between the pair, such as no alcohol being sold at all, in and outside of the ground, are almost unheard of in domestic English football rivalries. Apart from this one.

Chapter 2:

Born Out of the Docks

The birth of the modern day Millwall Football Club predates West Ham United by ten years, however, the wheels were set in motion for the founding of the Lions well before their founding in the mid-1880s. Entrepreneur John Thomas Morton established J.T. Morton in Aberdeen in 1849 as a food retailer. The company rapidly grew, becoming best known for preserving and canning foods. As a result of their success, J. T. Morton moved south of the border, setting up several locations in London in the 1850s. In 1872, Morton's opened a new plant on Westferry Road on the Isle of Dogs, taking over Price & Co's disused oil merchant site.

In 1885, the workers at J. T. Morton's had the bright idea of forming a football club for the workforce of the company. A common misconception throughout the years is that Millwall were originally a 'Scottish club' down south, due to the belief that workers from Morton's plants north of the border emigrated down to East London. In reality, the initial constitution of the newly formed Millwall Rovers were a make-up of English and Scottish members, with smatterings from the Emerald Isle - the club's first secretary, 17-year-old Jasper Sexton, was of Irish descent. Myths plague Millwall's early history. It's commonly believed the club's first chairman, William Murray-Leslie, was an Irish international footballer. He wasn't. Murray-Leslie, a doctor living in Manchester Road on the Isle of Dogs, was born in Knockbain in the north of Scotland, never turning out for an Irish representative team. One thing is true, there's certainly Scottish influence in the early days of Millwall's footballing heritage.

Millwall Rovers were born out of Iona, a distinctly Scottish name, who were an internal works team at Morton's factory. On 3 October 1885, playing in a distinctly Scottish blue and white, Millwall Rovers were downed 5-0 away to Leytonstone-based club Fillebrook in their first ever game. Not to be deterred, Millwall won their first home game, at Glengall Road, beating St Luke's 2-1. The history of Millwall's fervent and fanatic support was born that day, with a firework display and a street party being held at the Islanders Pub on Tooke Street, of which club secretary Sexton's father was the landlord. During Millwall Rovers' first season, the pub was also used as a club house and changing room for the club.

Rovers took to football like a duck to water, becoming the dominant club on the Isle of Dogs. Support grew for the club, forcing Millwall to move to the Lord Nelson Ground in 1886 and then onto the 20,000 capacity Athletic Grounds four years later at the expense of £500 (around £65,000 in today's money). After winning the East London Senior Cup three years in a row, the club became founder members of the Southern League in 1894, after turning professional a year prior. The success didn't stop there. The club, who had since been reconstituted and renamed to Millwall Athletic in 1889, won the first two editions of the Southern League in 1895 and 1896. Millwall's first Southern League success prompted the Football League to invite the club to the Second Division. Millwall rejected the offer, with the place going to Loughborough instead. After becoming the biggest club on the Isle of Dogs, Millwall were slowly starting to become a real force in London.

A mile or so east, another footballing revolution was brewing. Much like Millwall, West Ham United's history stretches way back before their 1895 formation. Formed in 1837, as the Ditchburn and Mare Shipbuilding Company, the Thames Ironworks and Shipbuilding Company stood on the banks of the River Lea in Canning Town. The company rapidly expanded, renaming to Thames Ironworks, building battleships for the country's war efforts. In the summer of 1895, it was decided by one-time England international and Thames Ironworks managing director Arnold Hills and company foreman Dave Taylor to set up an amateur team for the workers.

Within a few months of Thames Ironworks' birth, the club met a Millwall Athletic side for the first time on 3 December 1895 at Millwall's Athletic Grounds for a friendly. The trip to the Isle of Dogs wasn't a happy one for the newly formed club, Millwall's reserves dispatched the Irons with ease, winning 6-0, Thames Ironworks' biggest defeat in their inaugural season. The rivalry was set. Millwall Athletic drew a significant proportion of their support from the Millwall Iron Works, who were based at the south of the Isle of Dogs. The Millwall Iron Works were instrumental in changing attitudes towards labour in the country, introducing a half-day on Saturday, with workers finishing at 1pm. This new measure also helped the development of football in working class communities, freeing up bodies for the 3pm kick-off. Coincidentally, Millwall Iron Works were formed by Thames Ironworks founder Charles Mare in 1858. The two opposing ironwork companies regularly competed for business in the second half of the 19th century, leading to a rivalry between the two. The rivalry between the two were such that the two companies used different techniques in order to produce their final product. The intense feeling between West Ham and Millwall was alive, even before the two clubs were conceived.

Due to the cutthroat nature of late-Victorian football, Thames Ironworks' amateurism didn't last and the club turned professional three years later in 1898, upon joining the Southern League. The signs of Thames

Ironworks' amateurism were waning. In 1896, five players joined from Reading, with more external players joining in 1897.

"Millwall, even though away from home, should just about get through, though a hard game is certain."
The Standard, 8 December 1899

After their initial bout in 1895, the Thames Ironworks and Millwall Athletic met in a number of low-key friendlies, before finally meeting in a competitive game, being drawn together in the FA Cup fifth qualifying round on 9 December 1899. Millwall went into the tie as slight favourites, having reached the first round of the competition three years in a row. In front of a record crowd of 12,000 at Thames Ironworks' Memorial Grounds, a stadium itself billed as "good enough to stage an English cup final", Millwall Athletic ran out 2-1 winners. Hugh Goldie opened the scoring for Millwall inside ten minutes, before Thames Ironworks captain Harry Bradshaw equalised, scoring his final goal in football. Hugh Robertson scored the winner for Millwall before the half-time whistle, securing a place in the first round in the FA Cup for a fourth consecutive year for

Millwall. Millwall had ample opportunities to add to their lead in the second period, dominating proceedings in a wind-swept East London. Despite tasting defeat in the first competitive tie between the pair, losing was by no means a disgrace for Thames Ironworks, as Millwall marched on to the semi-finals of the competition, defeating eventual Football League champions Aston Villa after a replay along the way. Millwall were christened the Lions of the South by the national press, thanks to their cup exploits, with the nickname evolving into the club's current nickname of the Lions. The Lions eventually usurped the club's existing nickname of the Dockers – an obvious pointer to Millwall's heritage.

The theme of questionable weather continued for the second competitive meeting of the pair. Two days before Christmas Day in 1899, Millwall Athletic were 2-0 up in a Southern League tie at the Memorial Grounds with nineteen minutes remaining, before fog, rolling in from the banks of the Thames, forced the referee to abandon the tie, with the remainder to be played at a later date.

The Christmas period was not a happy one for the fleeting Thames Ironworks. In the midst of an eight-game losing streak that encompassed the whole of December, as well as the first half of January, the news was broke that Irons forward Harry Bradshaw had died. Bradshaw's health had been deteriorating since receiving a blow to the head from an opposition players' boot against Bedminster on 7 October 1899. Bradshaw managed to soldier on, playing the full 90 minutes in the next six of Thames Ironworks' fixtures, even managing to score in a 7-0 FA Cup trouncing away at Dartford, before his health issues got in the way. After missing Thames Ironworks' next two games against Swindon Town and Bristol City, Bradshaw made a scoring return in the cup tie against Millwall, before his clearly ailing health took precedence once again. Bradshaw passed away at his home in Tottenham in the afternoon on Christmas Day, being survived by his widow and two children.

Millwall and Thames Ironworks had to wait over four months to play the remaining 19 minutes of the abandoned December tie, first having to navigate another scheduled Southern League tie at the Athletic Grounds. Thames Ironworks' form had slowly been improving, putting four goals each past Southampton and Sheppey United in their two games prior before meeting Millwall. On a spring afternoon on the Isle of Dogs, the Irons ran out 1-0 winners, thanks to a strike from Scotsman Kenny McKay. Immediately after Thames Ironworks' maiden victory over their rivals, the final minutes of the thwarted festive tie was played out, with no further score.

Even in the early days of the two clubs, it was apparent games between the pair were attracting a level of interest that wasn't held for their other Southern League ties, with Thames Ironworks averaging gates of around 2,000 to 4,000 in the fledgling months of the 1899-00 season. This all changed when Millwall came to town in December, with another 10,000 being added to the gate. Two attendances of 5,000 at the Memorial Grounds were recorded in early April; these being the closest the Ironworks came to matching their attendances against their rivals on the Isle of Dogs.

Following the 1899-00 season, Thames Ironworks were wound up at the end of June, with a newly formed club, West Ham United, coming into existence on 5 July 1900, replacing Thames Ironworks in the Southern

League, inheriting a number of Ironworks' players and the Memorial Grounds. The Ironworks themselves had been in decline for quite some time, with the workforce being slashed in half from 1860 to 1900 as shipyards on the banks of the River Clyde and in the north east of England became the new homes of shipbuilding in the United Kingdom.

The rivalry was soon reignited, with the new West Ham United travelling to the Athletic Grounds to meet Millwall Athletic in West Ham's second competitive game of the 1900-01 campaign. Much like Thames Ironworks' first game against Millwall, the Lions ran out winners, winning 3-1, much against the run of play. On 22 December 1900, a sense of déjà vu was felt around the Memorial Grounds as another derby game was called off due to fog with twenty minutes remaining.

Prior to the game being replayed on 21 March 1901, rumblings of a decision that may have changed the face of English football were afoot. Due to West Ham's poor financial state and the relative early success of Millwall, talks of a merger between the two were on the cards, with the Memorial Grounds being touted as a potential new home for any new club. The replay, played under the cloud of a proposed merger, finished in a 1-0 victory for West Ham, with local lad Fred Corbett scoring a late, contentious winner. The weather? Awful.

Although the proposed merger was shelved, change was still in the air for both West Ham and Millwall ahead of the 1901-02 season. Charlie Dove, who played in well over 100 games for both Thames Ironworks and West Ham United, controversially left the club for Millwall after six years at West Ham and their previous incarnation. Also, on the move were Millwall themselves, leaving the Athletic Grounds for a site in North Greenwich a few hundred yards down the road. Millwall's eleven-year stay at the Athletic Grounds wasn't a particularly pretty one. Although the ground was remarked as one of the best in the south of England, as a result of mud getting dredged up from the nearby docks by the Millwall Freehold Land and Dock Company, a smell that "wouldn't come off for weeks" embedding itself into players' kits according to Fred Pelly, who won three caps for England, hung in the air. The adjacent area of Mudchute on the island took its name from the methods used next to Millwall's second home. Additionally, both clubs entered teams into London League and the Western League, making for more match-ups between the pair.

The Lions had the upper hand in the early days of the derby. From April 1902 to February 1904, Millwall set a number of records in the early history of the rivalry, including being unbeaten in 12 games across four competitions: the Southern League, the London League, the Western League and a Southern Professional Charity Cup semi-final tie, the latter of which saw the derby's biggest win – a 7-1 win for Millwall at the Memorial Grounds on 2 April 1903. Millwall were by far the most dominant team between the two in general during this era, helping themselves to a 6-0 home win against Queens Park Rangers just three days later. Millwall finished the 1902-03 season as FA Cup semi-finalists again, reaching this stage of the competition for the second time in three years. By contrast, West Ham's furthest foray in the competition by that point was the intermediate round in 1900-01 and 1902-03.

Ahead of the 1904-05 season, West Ham vacated the Memorial Grounds after seven years at the site, choosing to move just over a mile east to Upton Park, taking over local club Boleyn Castle's tenancy of the Boleyn Ground. Despite the Memorial Grounds' grand facilities, the ground wasn't practical for an ambitious West Ham United. The site sat in a pocket of East London largely unserved by public transport, due to the relatively low population density, with West Ham station only being completed halfway through West Ham's stay at the Memorial Grounds. By contrast, the Boleyn Ground stood in an area easily accessible on foot from the densely populated suburbs of East Ham, Plaistow and Upton Park. Additionally, Upton Park station had already served the area for over 25 years, with a tramway running down the Barking Road.

West Ham finally broke their duck against Millwall in historic circumstances, hosting the side for the inaugural game at the Boleyn. On 1 September 1904, hosted on a Thursday afternoon in front of a crowd of 10,000 spectators, West Ham blew away Millwall, brushing the Lions aside 3-0, thanks to a brace from local boy Billy Bridgeman and new signing Jack Flynn, scoring on his debut for the club. West Ham's victory, just their sixth in 24 games against Millwall, was largely attributed to the Hammers' transfer dealings in the summer by the national press. These new signings helped West Ham finish four places above Millwall in the Southern League, the first time the Hammers had achieved the feat of bettering their rivals in the league.

Meanwhile, crowd trouble had slowly been creeping in at football, with a pitch invasion in March 1905 against Brighton & Hove Albion overshadowing Brighton's 3-1 against West Ham win at the Goldstone Ground on the south coast. A September 1906 Western League meeting, coming five months after Millwall recorded their first win at the Boleyn Ground, helped light the blue touch paper in terms for spectator violence that would set the tone for the rivalry in later years. The *Stratford Express* reported that crunching tackles established the mood for the tie, before West Ham wing-half Len Jarvis sent Millwall's Alf Dean flying into an iron advertising hoarding, leading Dean to limp off the field of play, unable to continue. A George Kitchen penalty secured all three points for the Irons, before Millwall's George Comrie departed due to injury, forcing

Millwall to see out the rest of the game with nine men. The bad-tempered affairs on the pitch emanated onto the terraces, with the *East Ham Echo* reporting on fist fights behind the goals. As a result of scenes seen during the Monday afternoon tie, the Football Association ordered West Ham to put up warning notices around the Boleyn Ground to dissuade supporters from engaging in violence. Len Jarvis was also banned by the FA for a fortnight for his assault on Dean, with an FA commission set up to investigate the match labelling the tie as "far too vigorous", laying most of the blame on the referee for failing to control the tie.

More records were set in the springtime of 1909. Early Millwall icon Alf Twigg notched his tenth goal in the derby, scoring Millwall's only goal in a 5-1 London PFA Charity Fund win for the Hammers. It's looking increasingly unlikely that Twigg's record will remain untouched, especially considering the irregularity of games between the pair in the modern era. The pair played each other well over fifty times before World War I kicked off, compared to the rather paltry figure of 16 meetings from 1978 to 2012.

Another milestone, perhaps the most important, was yet to come. In 1910, Millwall swapped East London for South London, moving to the £10,000 purpose-built Den. Millwall's lifespan on the Isle of Dogs had long been looking precarious, due to the increasing inaccessibility of Millwall's home, due to the rising traffic around the area. Despite the move to South London, picking up new support in the process, Millwall still retained support from their old base on the Isle of Dogs, with the club's original support making the pilgrimage underneath the Thames, using the newly constructed Greenwich Foot Tunnel. Millwall's life in South London didn't get off to the best of starts, losing 1-0 against Brighton & Hove Albion on 22 October 1910, in front of a crowd of 25,000 and Lord Arthur Kinnaird, president of the FA. Such was the prestigious nature of Millwall's new home, the ground was deemed worthy enough to host an England international in March 1911 against Wales. England eased to a 3-0 victory at The Den. Funnily enough, West Ham forward George Webb scored on his debut for the Three Lions. By contrast, partly as a consequence of the construction of Wembley Stadium in the early 1920s, Upton Park wasn't chosen to host a full England international until

2003. Upon moving to South London, Millwall dropped the Athletic suffix from their name.

On 9 March 1912, the pair faced each other for the first time in a competitive fixture in the differing climates of New Cross. Millwall were ruthless, easily dispatching the Hammers 5-1, in front of a partisan crowd of 28,400, Millwall's biggest attendance they had experienced at The Den so far and the biggest gate the two had experienced in a derby match between them. By this point in time, the demographics of the two groups of supporters were beginning to change, as well. During the early 1910s, the Thames Ironworks and Shipbuilding Company's business was really slowing down, eventually leading to the shipyards' closure in December 1912. The closure led to a majority of the shipyards' workforce migrating, who were overwhelmingly West Ham supporters, to working in the Royal Docks. Similarly, as a result of their migration, Millwall were picking up new supporters in the workforce of the Surrey Commercial Docks, partly as a result of no major club having played in this pocket of South London. More fuel to add the fire.

Chapter 3:

The World at War

More drama and fighting were soon afoot. As a result of a Serb shooting an Austrian to death in Bosnia, the United Kingdom was eventually drawn into World War I, a conflict that would claim the lives of at least 20 million people. The war, which plunged the entire of Europe into uncertainty, had a profound effect on football, too. Due to the intensity of the conflict cranking up in the second half of 1914, a decision was made between the Football Association and the War Office to set up a Football Battalion in order to help the war effort. A number of Millwall and West Ham players made up the battalion. Due to the number of footballers fighting overseas, 'guesting' became the norm in English football during the war, a predecessor to the modern loan system. Another local war effort was that of the West Ham Pals, a 'pals battalion' set up in December

1914, officially known as the 13th (Service) Battalion of the Essex Regiment. The West Ham Pals, made up of local men from East London and Essex, stood toe-to-toe in the trenches alongside the Football Battalion. A cry of "Up the Hammers!" was the Pals' battle cry, before the battalion faced a devastating loss at the Battle of Cambrai in Northern France towards the back-end of 1917. The Pals' faced huge losses during the conflict, with around 250 of the original 1,000 men dying at war, with hundreds more facing physical or mental conditions due to the unforgiving nature of the Western Front.

With all the death and devastation, it's easy to forget that football was still being played back in Blighty. Millwall and West Ham soldiered on the Southern League in the early days of the war, recording respectable finishes at fourth and eighth place respectively. At the end of the 1914-15 season, the Southern League and the FA Cup were put on hold, as it was becoming apparent the war would last longer than the few months the public had initially believed. Football was regionalised for the remainder of the war, with Millwall and West Ham entering the London Combination alongside eleven other clubs from the capital. The pair fared well in the first edition of the Combination, with Millwall finishing second, two places ahead of the Hammers in fourth, quite a feat, considering they were competing alongside a number of Football League clubs, higher up the footballing pyramid. Even better was to come for the clubs in the following season with West Ham United topping the London Combination, scoring 110 goals along the way, with Millwall finishing runners-up.

The Great War, as it was then known, hit close to home for both clubs, with several players on the books for the two dying in the conflict. They are as follows:

Millwall
Joe Dines
Born: 12 April 1886; King's Lynn, United Kingdom
Died: 27 September 1918; Pas-de-Calais, France
Rank: Second-lieutenant

Charles Green
Born: 2 February 1888; Deptford, United Kingdom
Died: 1 November 1917; Passendale, Belgium
Rank: Private

George Porter
Born: 24 May 1891; Horsham, United Kingdom
Died: 14 July 1918; Hauts-de-France, France
Rank: Lance Corporal

John Williams
Born: 15 February 1885; Buckley, United Kingdom
Died: 5 June 1916; Arras, France
Rank: Private

West Ham United
Arthur Stallard
Born: September 1892; Hackney, United Kingdom
Died: 30 November 1917; Cambrai, France
Rank: Private

Although the above players died in the conflict whilst actively playing for Millwall and West Ham, a number of ex-players also met their end on the battlefields of France and Belgium, with countless other players, current and former, picking up career-ending injuries whilst at war. In reality, you'd probably be hard-pressed to find a football club during this era that didn't experience some sort of loss during this time.

Following World War I, normal football was resumed with the Football League undergoing an expansion, with West Ham United joining Coventry City, Port Vale, Rotherham County, South Shields and Stoke in the Second Division in 1919. West Ham were growing, hitting a new attendance high of 30,000 in March 1920 in a 2-1 win against Tottenham Hotspur. The year after West Ham's election into the Football League, it was Millwall's turn to enter, joining the newly established Third Division alongside 20 other newly elected clubs.

The election of both clubs into the Football League breathed new life into the pair. Firstly, West Ham reached heady heights in 1923, navigating five rounds to reach the FA Cup final, the first to be held at the newly built Wembley Stadium. Despite losing 2-0 to favourites Bolton Wanderers, the final will forever live in English football folklore, being nicknamed the White Horse Final, after a sole white horse helped clear the pitch after thousands of fans flooded the playing surface, with estimates ranging from 200,000 to 300,000 spectators packing inside Wembley on the April afternoon. A strong finish to the season also saw West Ham gain promotion to the Football League First Division for the first time in their history, just a mere four years after they were elected to the Football League. Millwall, themselves, were enjoying a healthy period, setting a joint-record Football League run of eleven games without conceding in the second half of the 1925-26 season, winning nine. Despite their astute defence towards the end of the season, Millwall were unable to gain promotion from the Third Division, losing more away games than they won, nine to seven. The tide for success had turned in the rivalry, however, with West Ham firmly the most successful club during the 1920s, after Millwall's domination during the very early 20th century.

The general strike of 1926 helped set the tone in later years for the ill-feeling. Another dimension of the rivalry that is shrouded in more myth than fact, the truth has never fully been established and a large proportion of both fanbases still believe that Millwall supporting dockers broke picket lines, whilst the West Ham supporters working in the docks remained strong, striking until the end. The facts are as follows: on 4 May 1926, a general strike was called by the Trades Union

Congress in solidarity with a million coal miners who were prevented from working after a dispute arose with the owners of the coal miners over conditions, pay and working hours. The strike was well supported within the working class, with railway workers, factory workers, ironworkers and dockers being just some of the 1.5 million labourers refusing to work. The last tradesmen listed, dockers, is pertinent to the legend that has arisen. As previously mentioned, the London dockers were mostly of either a West Ham or Millwall persuasion, with Millwall still retaining a healthy level of support of the Isle of Dogs, despite vacating the island 16 years previous, as well as in South London. This is about as far as the myth of the general strike goes. At the Surrey Commercial Docks in Rotherhithe, only a handful of people turned up for work, out of the 2,000 strong workforce. Similarly, up the road from Millwall's first few homes on the Isle of Dogs, the striking workers helped bring forward the closure of the Millwall Extension Railway line by over a month. This sent out a clear message that the dockers in London stood shoulder-to-shoulder with their comrades in the coal industry. The strike was ultimately unsuccessful. One theory behind the myth of Millwall working and West

Ham striking is that the docks north and south of the Thames were rivals themselves, in direct competition for trade. Although an interesting belief, it's also untrue. The Port of London Authority was formed in 1909, taking control of all of the docks in London, ending the quarrelling. A similar myth exists on the south coast, with Portsmouth fans labelling Southampton supporters "scummers" (a term again shrouded in the myth and mists of the docks) for apparently breaking a strike during the 1930s. There's no hard evidence for widespread strike action on the docks on the south coast in this period, let alone breaking the picket lines.

Back to football, more success for Millwall was to follow in 1928, gaining promotion from the Third Division South, owing a big part of their triumph to their superb home record – nineteen wins, two draws and zero losses, being just one of two clubs in the entire Football League not to lose a home game in the league in the 1927-28 season, the other being Third Division North club Stockport County.

Thanks to their accomplishments in the 1920s, West Ham United had escaped the Lions' grasp, with the two clubs only meeting in the London Challenge Cup and the London PFA Charity Fund; neither competition captured the imagination of the East End, with meagre attendances of just a few thousand being the norm. After impressive wins in the fourth round against Leeds United and Doncaster Rovers respectively, West Ham and Millwall were drawn together in the fifth round of the FA Cup, a tie to be played at Upton Park on 15 February 1930. The Lions came into the tie as the only Second Division club not to record an away win all season. Forest Gate born striker Vivian Gibbins, who still played for West Ham on amateur terms, opened the scoring on 17 minutes. Millwall slowly grew into the tie, before three goals in four minutes, mostly against the run of play according to *The Guardian's* match report on the Monday morning, condemned Millwall to an early exit. Millwall did score three minutes into the second period, however, the late West Ham onslaught in the first half, not helped by goalkeeper Joe Lansdale's errors, proved too much for the South Londoners to deal with.

The first Football League meeting between the pair was not far off. West Ham finished the 1931-32 First Division season in shambolic fashion, losing nine out of their last ten games, conceding 37 goals in the process, finishing bottom and being relegated at the end of the campaign. Millwall were plodding along just fine, finishing eighth in the Second Division. The Hammers came into the 1932-33 season in the same fashion they left the previous one in: dismally; conceding fifteen goals in their opening five games. Millwall, coming into the game off the back of a 2-0 win the previous week against Lincoln City, were humbled by an out of sorts West Ham, in front of an official crowd of 25,496 (however, newspaper reports from the time estimated thousands more were in attendance), thanks to a brace from club record goal scorer Vic Watson and a strike from John Morton.

Millwall didn't have to wait long to get their own back on West Ham, winning 1-0 at The Den in front of an uncharacteristically seasonal low crowd of 4,063 on 31 January 1933 – the low attendance owing to the last-minute rescheduling of the game due to Millwall's FA Cup commitments. The win kick-started a six-game unbeaten streak for the Lions, allowing the club to finish the season in a respectable position of seventh, the club's highest finish since being elected into the Football

League. The Hammers finished the season in 20th place, just one point above safety, their lowest ever finish to date. The season will go down in infamy for the Hammers not only for their lowly finish, but also for the way manager Syd King's departure from the club came about. King, who had been suffering from delusions and paranoia towards the end of his tenure, had turned to alcohol to try and remedy his problems, being drunk on official club time on one more than one occasion. A month after his contract was officially terminated by West Ham, King committed suicide in February 1933. An undignified ending for a man who had given 33 years of service to West Ham as a player, secretary and manager.

The following season, on 21 October 1933, a record attendance between the pair at The Den of 28,080 saw Millwall storm into a 2-0 lead, thanks, in no small part, to a double from Laurie Fishlock, before West Ham pegged the Lions back. Vic Watson started off the comeback, before West Ham stalwart Jim Barrett converted a penalty to spare the Hammers' blushes. Attendance figures had been improving during the 1930s. A record reported crowd between West Ham and

Millwall of 41,300 watched the two battle it out on 27 December 1938 at Upton Park. The crowd packing into the Boleyn Ground were treated to a thriller – a 0-0 draw, the first between the two in 21 years. The game must have been so action-packed that newspapers in Canada and the United States were wired through that the game was postponed. One man who seemingly made a good impression, though, was West Ham outside-right Stan Foxall, who courted a £4,000 bid from Millwall manager Charlie Hewitt immediately after the draw. West Ham rejected the bid without a second thought.

The good times, however, would not roll. Following Germany's invasion of Poland on 1 September 1939, the United Kingdom and France declared war on Germany two days later. The war was brewing in Europe for a while. Following West Ham's 2-1 win at home against Fulham on 28 August 1939, a number of Hammers players were ordered to report to their position as air raid wardens. A day before the outbreak of war, soldiers stood on the terraces to watch Leicester City gun down West Ham 2-0 at Upton Park, with barrage balloons hovering above the East London skyline. Three days after the declaration of war, the Football League season was scrapped, with players' contracts and season tickets being cancelled. Much like World War I, Millwall and West Ham entered a special wartime competition – the Football League South. Attendances were down during the Second World War, due to the constant threat of the Luftwaffe's raids on the Docklands and restrictions regarding capacity numbers in wartime Britain. Despite this, 42,399 spectators turned out at Wembley Stadium to witness West Ham win the inaugural Football League War Cup, beating Blackburn Rovers 1-0. The new wartime competitions made for some interesting results, including West Ham beating Millwall 7-5 at Upton Park on 14 November 1942.

Despite all the fun and games, the reality of war was still lurking and this became all too apparent for both clubs. In the wee hours of the new week on 14 April 1943, Millwall's Den was the victim of a Luftwaffe bombing, resulting in a large crater in the North Terrace, scattering concrete and crush barriers across the pitch. The Den was always under the threat of Germany's scourge, sitting just a mile away from the Surrey Commercial Docks. Twelve days later, the Lions suffered a bigger blow to their stadium. Following the final whistle on an Easter Monday London Senior Cup final tie between Dulwich Hamlet and Tooting & Mitcham United at The Den, a fire quickly engulfed Millwall's wooden Main Stand, destroying the structure in 30 minutes, arguably causing more devastation to the club that Hitler's Luftwaffe could've ever achieved. West Ham offered their help to their neighbours south of the Thames and for a period of ten months, Millwall played their games at Upton Park, as well as using the grounds of Charlton Athletic and Crystal Palace.

Bill Voisey, Millwall's manager, was severely injured in the air raid, retiring from his post as manager in November 1944 as a result of the injuries sustained in the bombing. Voisey was as Millwall as they come. Born on the Isle of Dogs, Voisey's family lived down Manchester Road on the island, much like a number of early Millwall staff members, with Voisey's sister, Alice, working in J. T. Morton's factory, where the club were formed. Voisey began his association with Millwall in 1908, after playing for several smaller clubs on the Isle of Dogs. The full-back played for Millwall for fifteen years, earning an unofficial cap with England in 1919 along the way. Following his retirement from the game, Voisey took up the post of Millwall manager in 1940, after managing the Great Britain football team during the 1936 Olympic Games. Not to be deterred by old age, Voisey made a final appearance for the club in May 1941, at the grand age of 50, in a London War Cup tie against none other than West Ham.

The Islanders Pub, used all those years ago when Millwall played on the Isle of Dogs, was also destroyed by a German air raid in September 1940. The pub, which was never rebuilt, stood strong for 90 years before the attack. Tooke Street, where the pub stood, was later consigned to history, being bulldozed in slum clearances two decades later.

Just over a year on from the attack on The Den, West Ham's Boleyn Ground came under attack from a V-1 flying bomb, destroying the majority of the South Bank and a portion of the West Stand in August 1944. Undeterred by the destruction, West Ham recorded nine consecutive wins whilst playing away from Upton Park, before returning to East London in December. Miraculously, no deaths were recorded in either of the raids at Millwall and West Ham. Prime Minister Winston

Churchill praised the East London populace for staying strong in the face of adversity. East London responded by voting Churchill out of office in the immediate aftermath of the war.

The 1940s petered out with a few meetings: a 3-1 win for West Ham United in the Second Division, followed by three draws in a row between the pair in 1947 in the second tier.

Chapter 4:
Time Apart

They say absence makes the heart grow stronger. After meeting over 75 times since their formation until the end of the 1940s, the duo only faced each other once in a competitive first team meeting in the 1950s – a 3-1 win for West Ham in the Southern Floodlit Cup in 1959. Going into the 1950s, the gap between West Ham and Millwall was widening, with more of a disparity between the two than ever before. With the exception of the Southern Floodlit Cup tie in '59, the two clubs only met in reserve games in the London Mid-Week League and the South East Counties League during the 1950s, with the pair not facing each other at all during the 1960s in a competitive game – the only decade the two haven't met since their formation in the 19th century.

In 1948, Millwall finished rock bottom of the Second Division, being relegated back into the Third Division South. Ten years later, more heartbreak was to follow for the Lions, becoming founder members of the newly created Fourth Division, following a depressing 23rd place finish in the Third Division South. The regional Third Divisions were wound up at the end of the 1957-58 season, after Britain got back on track following the Second World War, with the economic reasons for regionalising the Football League becoming less apparent.

The Hammers, on the other hand, were slowly, but surely, on the up again. Following 26 years without First Division football, West Ham were finally promoted back into the first tier of English football in 1958, clinching promotion in emphatic fashion, recording 5-0, 6-1 and 8-0 wins against Stoke City, Lincoln City and Rotherham United respectively.

By the end of the 1958-59 season, three divisions and seventy league places separated the two clubs, with Millwall exiting the FA Cup at the second round stage to non-league club Worcester City, who would later overcome Liverpool in the next stage.

The lack of meetings between Millwall and West Ham forced the pair into scouring the capital for other derby games. Millwall got lucky, regularly competing in the same competitions as fellow South Londoners Crystal Palace. Millwall's old Den sat just under six miles away, as the crow flies, from Palace's Selhurst Park. The Glaziers, as Palace used to be known as in the '50s, and the Lions met nineteen times between September 1950 and October 1958, with Palace failing to win a single game against Millwall. Things just weren't the same, however. Despite meeting each other 23 times competitively during the 1950s and both being south of the river, there was never any real feeling of 'hatred' between the two, probably owing to the lack of history that Crystal Palace and Millwall had between each other, as well as their contrasting fanbases. Closer to The Den, Millwall finally met Charlton Athletic in 1966, after 31 years without facing each other. Much like their meetings with Crystal Palace, the Lions' bouts with Charlton failed to live up to the hype they'd had with West Ham. According to the 2003 Football Fans

Census, Millwall regarded both Crystal Palace and Charlton as their second and third biggest rivalries respectively.

West Ham had a harder time looking for local rivals, with Leyton Orient being the only other East London club to compete in the Football League prior to Dagenham & Redbridge's promotion into League Two in 2007. In October 1956, 34 years after last meeting each other in the Second Division, West Ham and Leyton Orient met at Orient's Brisbane Road home, with the Hammers running out 2-1 winners, thanks to an own goal and a strike from Malcolm Musgrove. The rivalry between the two was purely competitive, with no real animosity between the two. During the less sectarian days of football support, it was known for West Ham supporters to adopt Orient as a 'second team', taking trips to Brisbane Road when the Hammers were away. The two played each other in Orient's only stint in the First Division in the 1962-63 season. Orient won the first meeting 2-0, their first ever win in the top flight of English football, in front of 23,918 at Brisbane Road on 1 September 1962. Although it would look good for Orient in the present day, the attendance figure wasn't an anomaly for the club in the early '60s, suggesting there was no real rivalry between the two. Leyton Orient would only win five more league games that season, finishing rock bottom of the First Division. Orient haven't come close to tasting top-flight football since. As a sidenote, in recent years, relations between West Ham and Leyton Orient have become frayed due to former Orient chairman Barry Hearn's pursuit for the Olympic Stadium – a site that West Ham moved into in the summer of 2016. Hearn probably didn't help proceedings with his comments saying West Ham should be "petrified" of Orient under their new owner Francesco Becchetti. Under Becchetti's ownership, Orient were relegated into non-league for the first time in their history.

The 1960s were a period of all change for football fan culture in England. Firstly, Millwall's 3:15pm kick-offs were scrapped in favour of kicking-off fifteen minutes earlier, with the FA wanting to kick-offs to be more uniformed across the Football League. As is well established, Millwall's fanbase had a strong core of dock workers. Newport County and Plymouth Argyle were also allowed to kick-off at 3:15pm, as a concession to their dockyard support. The first signs of what we now regard as hooliganism were also beginning to creep into the game during the '60s. Millwall's support had always courted controversy, stretching back to 1919, when the programme notes at Millwall were forced to instruct the club's support to stop swearing, in fear of offending the "ladies" who attended games. After seeing The Den closed by the FA multiple times, in 1920, 1934, 1948 and 1950, due to crowd disturbances, it was time for Millwall to be fully demonised by the British press in 1965. On 6 November 1965, on a trip across town to Brentford, a member of Millwall's away support had the ingenious idea of hurling an imitation hand grenade towards Brentford's goalkeeper Chic Brodie. The incident was like a red rag to a bull, with the British tabloids sensationalising the event, likening a grenade in the goalmouth to a warzone. The actual warzone scenes of fighting on the terraces and Millwall 'keeper Alex Stepney, later a European Cup winner with Manchester United, being kicked and pelted with glass bottles were conveniently left out. That didn't matter, the British press had found a scapegoat for their societal problems in Millwall, a reputation that Millwall have never been able to fully shake off. After a day of violence in football stadia across the country on that cold November day, *The Guardian* asked "When are these disgraceful outbursts to end? How are the rowdies to be curbed?" This was just the start.

Back on the pitch, both teams experienced *anni mirabiles* during the mid-'60s. After suffering relegation back into the fourth tier in 1964, Millwall kicked on under the management of Billy Gray, securing two successive promotions. There had been concern in the Millwall boardroom that staying in the Fourth Division could have disastrous consequences for the future of the club. The club were already in a precarious position, with Millwall chairman Micky Purser and his car showroom down the Old Kent Road taking the brunt of the fans' frustration for not fulfilling their potential.

Amid Millwall climbing back up into the Second Division for the first time in 18 years, the Hammers were experiencing the best era in their history. Led by England captain Bobby Moore, West Ham embarked on a period of unprecedented success. In 1964, West Ham lifted the FA Cup for the first ever time, overcoming Preston North End by three goals to two at Wembley

Stadium. As a consequence of the club winning the FA Cup, the club entered the European Cup Winners' Cup the following season, successfully navigating four rounds, before coming up against DFB-Pokal winners 1860 München, again at Wembley Stadium, in front of 100,000 spectators. West Ham won the final 2-0, thanks to two late goals from Alan Sealey. 1966, however, was West Ham's crowning moment. After a passable season, finishing 12th in the Football League, getting to the final of the League Cup and the semi-finals of the Cup Winners' Cup, the club's moment in the sun came on 30 July 1966. Captained by Bobby Moore, England ran out 4-2 winners after extra time against West Germany in the World Cup final, with a hat-trick from Sir Geoff Hurst and one from Sir Martin Peters, both West Ham forwards, leading the *Stratford Express* to christen West Ham as World Cup winners – a tag that West Ham supporters still hold dear to this day.

Chapter 5:

The Dawn of Hooliganism

No sooner than seeing the swinging sixties end, did the not-so-savoury seventies come in. The 1970s saw a period of huge social and political upheaval in Britain. Bloody Sunday, the Three-Day Week and the election of Margaret Thatcher all helped shape the 70s into one of the most divisive and warped eras the country has ever witnessed.

Millwall started off the decade well. At the end of the 1971-72 season, the Lions were on the verge of tasting First Division football for the first time in the club's history. At the end of April, a professional, routine 2-0 home win, for Millwall against Preston North End put the Lions within touching distance of promotion – the fourth time in the club's Football League history they had completed a league season unbeaten at home. Confusion filled the South London air and Millwall's support flooded the pitch in the belief their closest promotion challengers, Birmingham City, had lost up north away to Sheffield Wednesday. They hadn't. Ecstasy turned to agony after the real result at Hillsborough began to filter through to The Den.

Birmingham finished the job on the following Tuesday night away to Orient, a single Bob Latchford goal being enough to take Birmingham back into the First Division, condemning Millwall to another season without their dream. Amongst the 33,383 strong crowd packed into Brisbane Road that night, there was a sizable contingent of Millwall supporters, in hope, more than expectation, that their London neighbours could do them a favour by winning and sealing promotion for the Lions. After it was becoming apparent that Birmingham would be going up, a number of Millwall fans invaded the pitch in an ambitious attempt to get the game abandoned, the result voided and Millwall's promotion confirmed. With a decent number of West Ham supporters inside Brisbane Road that night, violence was inevitable, with pockets of fighting breaking out throughout the night. One final twist on that mild May evening was a bomb scare at full-time, with supporters scrambling out the Main Stand on the demand of Orient's tannoy announcer Keith Simpson. No chances were to be taken, especially considering the Irish Republic Army had been involved in over 50 incidents thus far in 1972. In bemusement to the scare, Millwall's support immediately christened themselves the "MRA" in an impromptu chant. No prizes for guessing what that stood for. The only bombshell dropped that night was the fact Millwall were to be consigned to another season without First Division football.

Club legend Harry Cripps wore the armband for Millwall during the 71-72 season, gleefully proclaiming the club had, in fact, achieved promotion at full-time against Preston, amid the swathes of supporters embracing him, only for Millwall's world to come crashing down. 'Arry Boy, as he was lovingly called at The Den, was Millwall to the core. A no-nonsense full-back with an eye for goal, the Millwall support fed off of Cripps' fiery nature, in turn pushing Cripps to perform like he was in the First Division.

It was only fair that Cripps was awarded a testimonial. After all, he would later go on to break Millwall's club record for the most Football League appearances. West Ham United were the club chosen to help honour Cripps' service to

Millwall. Moving down to East London from Norfolk as a young boy, the Hammers spotted Cripps' abilities, tying him down to their academy. Cripps would sign professional terms for the Hammers, making his debut in a Southern Floodlit Cup for the club in 1959 against Millwall of all teams. Cripps failed to make another appearance for West Ham, later signing for Millwall in 1961. After 25 years of not meeting each other at The Den, a decidedly different concoction of West Ham supporters made the trip down to South London than had travelled down in the immediate post-war era. On a chilly Thursday night south of the Thames, football hooliganism reared its ugly head in the most shocking of circumstances. Moments before kick-off, a sizeable number of West Ham's support attempted to storm Millwall's Cold Blow Lane terrace, where Millwall's most hardened of supporters stood, resulting in running battles for the rest of the night. Glass bottles, knives, darts and snooker balls were amongst some of the weapons used as New Cross resembled the Battle of the Somme more than a football stadium. In scenes frequently described as "pure evil", eighteen people were injured after a crush barrier buckled underneath the weight of the conflict unfolding in the Cold Blow Lane end. Ask any of the 10,000 crowd what happened during the game and you'd be hard-pressed to find anyone who remembers anything about what happened on the pitch, such was the fascination and fear with what was developing on the terraces. West Ham ran out 5-3 winners on a night where the result was definitely the second thought of most at The Den, with fights raging on in the South London night for over three hours. Amazingly, there were no fatalities that night, quite a feat considering weapons used and the amount of blood flowing down the terraces and in the surrounding streets. There's definitely an argument to be made that the events at Cripps' testimonial helped ignite the modern rivalry between the two clubs that we all know today.

Amazingly, the events at Cripps' testimonial didn't seem to put Millwall's board off, and just two years later, on 3 December 1974, Millwall once again invited West Ham down to The Den for Billy Neil's testimonial. What's even more baffling about the organisation of Neil's testimonial is that Neil was a Scot with zero connection to West Ham. The Hammers won another testimonial thriller 4-3 on a night where violence was, once again, the main point of conversation at The Den. By chance, Cripps himself was present at The Den for Neil's testimonial, despite leaving for rivals Charlton two months earlier, turning out for an ex-Millwall XI team against a Jimmy Hill XI before the main event. Bizarrely, Millwall's matchday programme labelled West Ham as their "very good friends". Probably the last time the two would be called friends, let alone very good friends. Millwall and West Ham would never play each other in a friendly again.

The renewing of tensions and hatred came to a head of the night of 21 September 1976, becoming a black night in not only the history of the rivalry, but in the history of both Millwall and West Ham all together, despite the pair not playing against each other. West Ham were down in South London to play Charlton in a League Cup third round tie in front of a bumper crowd of 32,898, a significant boost from the Addicks' last home game eleven days prior against Luton Town that drew a paltry attendance figure of 9,191. The declared attendance figure that night was a rather conservative figure, given most estimates for that night's gate put the figure more around the 50,000 mark. Trouble that night was always brewing, even at The Valley. Six people were arrested during and after a 1-0 West Ham win, with a policeman receiving injuries to his kidneys after being kicked whilst on the floor. Paul Cronin, a 21-year-old Charlton supporter from Kent, was attacked by a 20-strong gang of West Ham fans at full-time, leaving him in a coma. Upon awakening, the newly married Cronin suffered from amnesia and a speech defect.

At the same time as West Ham battling it out with Charlton, Millwall were at home to Orient, playing out a 0-0 draw in the same competition. To get back to East London, West Ham had to travel, via rail, through Millwall's heartland of New Cross in order to get back to Central London to change onto the District Line back home. Millwall's fans, beginning to filter out from The Den after their clash against Orient, lay in wait for West Ham's support at New Cross. At 9:55pm that evening, tragedy struck. 18-year-old Millwall supporter Ian Pratt was an unemployed labourer living on the Adams Garden Estate in Rotherhithe, who had been at Millwall's home game that evening. What happened next is as unclear today as it was on that night and the true truth will probably never be uncovered. The facts are as follows: at New Cross station, Millwall and West Ham fans battled on the platforms and on the trains, engaging in 'scarf-stealing' – a common practice at the time. Pratt allegedly attempted to steal a West Ham supporters' scarf before moving between one carriage from the other, either falling or being pushed onto the tracks below the hurtling locomotive, being killed instantly. A number of West Ham supporters were sought out by the police, but were never found, with investigators never being able to conclude what happened that night in New Cross. A single West Ham scarf was found next to his mutilated body on the track, alongside Pratt's Millwall scarf.

Hooliganism was firmly in the public's conscience by this point and football and hooliganism were increasingly becoming inseparable. In November 1977, the name of Millwall Football Club was permanently blackened in the British psyche. Journalist Charles Wheeler and the BBC took their cameras down to The Den on the behest of Millwall manager Gordon Jago to film a *Panorama* documentary in an attempt to convince the nation that Millwall's fanbase wasn't full of mindless thugs intent on violence. Since his appointment three years earlier, Jago had been on a mission to clean up Millwall's name with newly appointed chairman Herbert Burnige, however, the *Panorama* piece, broadcast on prime-time television, proved a step too far for Jago, who resigned the following month. The BBC documentary was a disaster for the club, with larger-than-life caricatures labelling themselves Harry the Dog and Bobby the Wolf bringing shame upon the club, recounting tales of violence and blasting threats at *Panorama's* cameras aimed at opposition supporters. Wheeler introduced the public to three groups that patrolled the terraces at The Den: The Halfway Line (the firm of choice for the younger generation), Treatment (who, somewhat bizarrely, were known to wear surgical gowns and face masks on the terraces) and F-Troop (Harry and Bobby's go-to group, whom Wheeler described as "the real nutters"). Perhaps most damning of all for the club was *Panorama* linking the club's fanbase to the fascist National Front. Neo-Nazi Martin Webster was interviewed by the BBC for the programme, claiming The Den was the perfect place to distribute the fascist magazine *Bulldog* to match-goers. In truth, the majority of clubs in the capital were recipients of visits from the National Front at one point during the '70s, these visits just didn't happen to be broadcast on national television. Millwall, the police and the FA condemned the programme and attempted to stop the BBC from broadcasting it, fearing it would glamourise football violence and make Millwall an unfair target to opposing supporters. By the end of the '70s and continuing into the '80s, the Bushwackers were the firm most commonly associated with Millwall. The phrase bushwhacking comes from the various wars across the Atlantic in the USA in the 1700s and 1800s, in which bushwhackers engaged in ambushes and guerrilla warfare. Somewhat apt.

The majority of Football League clubs during the 1970s and '80s had at least one firm. Long before the idea of the Inter City Firm, the firm associated with West Ham that gained the most prominence, West Ham already had a number of small firms during football hooliganisms' relative infancy, such as the Canning Town Snipers, Mile End Mob, Teddy Bunter Firm and the Under Fives to name just a few.

The increase of hooliganism led Millwall to install fences at The Den, with disorder at an FA Cup tie with Ipswich Town forcing Millwall's hand. Fighting broke out on the terraces, before spilling onto the field of play and continuing in the streets around the ground after full-time after Millwall were thrashed 6-1 in the quarter-finals by future England manager Bobby Robson's side, with Robson's wish for flamethrowers to be turned on the Millwall support being broadcast by *Match of the Day*.

Fences began to pop up on the terraces and around the perimeter of pitches across the country, with fences on the terraces going up on West Ham's South Bank terrace in the late '70s to help segregate home and away supporters in the heyday of football violence. In the aftermath of the Hillsborough disaster in 1989, a bit of common sense prevailed and perimeter fencing was uninstalled en masse, albeit much too late to prevent disaster.

Millwall and West Ham had been warring against each other during the 1970s without meeting each other. In 1978, West Ham suffered relegation from the First Division, just three years after clinching their second FA Cup. Living in wait for the Hammers were Millwall, who had regained their Second Division status in 1976, thanks to the management of the aforementioned Jago.

On 7 October 1978, nineteen years after their last competitive meeting, West Ham hosted Millwall at Upton Park. As opposed to West Ham sitting pretty in sixth place, the Lions had endured a terrible start to the season. After a promising 2-1 win against Newcastle United on the opening day of the league season, Millwall's form had capitulated, losing five out of their next seven league games, including a League Cup defeat away to Brighton. As a result of the previous episodes between the pair in the '70s, tensions were incredibly high. In the weeks leading up to the derby, leaflets were distributed at Millwall's home matches and along the Old Kent Road calling for a West Ham supporter's death and a "day of hatred" in order to "avenge" Ian Pratt's death two years earlier. The authorities took no chance, drafting in the first police helicopter for an English football fixture and 500 Metropolitan Police officers, the largest police presence English football had ever seen at this point in history. Police separated the South Bank at the Boleyn with dogs in a heated atmosphere that saw 70 arrests and 25 spectators injured, including six police officers. Fights raged in the streets before, during and after the game, with scores of weapons, including railway spikes, knives and blocks of wood, with nails crudely sticking, out being seized by the police. After being kept back in Upton Park for 30 minutes following full-time, allowing as many West Ham supporters to disperse from the area as possible, Millwall were kettled back to Upton Park station via a police escort. It looks as if the Millwall pamphleteers got their revenge after an unidentified West Ham supporter, at least in the public eye, was stabbed to death with a knitting needle. Reports about this incident are sketchy at best, however, it wouldn't have been the first death due to football hooliganism in the 1978-79 season, after 21-year-old Chelsea supporter Vernon Brown was crushed to death by an oncoming bus at Chelsea's away game at Birmingham City in September after clashes in the streets. As is normally the case when West Ham and Millwall come up against each other, the actual football was just a sidenote to the main events of the day. If you were wondering, West Ham ran out 3-0 winners in front of a crowd of 22,210, thanks to a hat-trick from Bryan 'Pop' Robson.

With Millwall's Second Division status hanging by a thread, the duo met at The Den on 14 May 1979 – the first competitive meeting in South London between the pair since 1947. The Hammers' Second Division status was already confirmed for another season; an indifferent end of the season failed to nudge West Ham into one of the three promotion places. Helicopters were out in force again following the events in October, with clashes at Bank Underground station during the morning being the only real form of disorder throughout the day. The Met Police would've thanked their lucky stars the events of earlier on in the season didn't repeat themselves. Fan favourite Pop Robson once again opened the scoring for West Ham in front of a crowd of 11,968 in South London, before a spirited Millwall comeback, thanks to strikes from Dave Mehmet and Nicky Chatterton kept Millwall's survival hopes alive. After seeing two games postponed in February due to poor weather, including the return game against West Ham that was due to take place on 14 February 1979, Millwall had two games remaining in May to try and stay in the division, needing maximum points to ensure survival. The Lions only picked up one point and dropped back down to the Third Division.

The increase in hooliganism at Millwall and West Ham deterred away fans from travelling down to away games at The Den and Upton Park respectively, due to the risk of violence. Famously, just fourteen Liverpool supporters made up the 40,256 crowd at Upton Park for a 0-0 draw in February 1975 – a fact Everton supporters still use as a stick to beat their Merseyside rivals with, even to this day.

Chapter 6:
Tensions Come To A Head

By the 1980s, hooliganism, Millwall and West Ham United were in a perverse love triangle. As a result of winning their third FA Cup in 1980, West Ham once again represented England in the European Cup Winners' Cup. The Hammers' first foray into European competition in four years saw the club meet Castilla, Real Madrid's reserve team. Losing 3-1 in front of 40,000 spectators at Real Madrid's Estadio Santiago Bernabéu, West Ham's name was tarnished on the European continent; not for footballing reasons. Violence raged in Madrid and a West Ham supporter lost his life after being crushed by a bus up against a wall in the Spanish capital. The driver was never prosecuted. Hammers captain Billy Bonds, who had lifted the FA Cup at Wembley a few months prior, attracted some rare criticism from the club's support after labelling the disorderly fans in Madrid as "animals" and "scum" in a column in *The Sun*. Eyewitness accounts from the West Ham support on a fateful night in Madrid described Spain's Guardia Civil police force as particularly heavy-handed – an account that been retold various times by English football fans visiting Spain since. The return leg, in which West Ham overturned their deficit and progressed into the next round, was ordered to be played behind closed doors at Upton Park by UEFA. The only real disorder that night was the Castilla team coach coming under attack temporarily on the A13 on its way to Upton Park.

In the spring of 1981, Millwall and West Ham faced each other in the Southern Junior Floodlit Cup, in a two legged tie. As was to be expected by anybody familiar with the derby by now, a larger crowd turned out for the tie. Travelling down to The Den, a large contigent of West Ham supporters got on the the tube at Mile End and Whitechapel, eager at the thought of meeting their fiercest rivals for the first time in two years. As usual, you can imagine what happened – just not on the scale that was seen for first team matches.

This was all part of what the media dubbed "the English disease". If hooliganism was a disease, then in March

1985 life support was needed. A Wednesday evening FA Cup quarter-final paired Luton Town and Millwall together for a chance to play reigning English champions Everton in the semis. The bad feeling in the air was in the air from the second Millwall touched down in Luton as thousands of Millwall fans rampaged through the town centre, destroying anything in sight on the way to Luton's Kenilworth Road home. After forcing entry to the Kenilworth Stand via a broken turnstile, the away end was heaving from an uncharacteristically large Millwall following. The hooligan element in Millwall's following set upon the Luton Town support before, during and after the tie, during which Luton forward Brian Stein scored the only goal of the game, leading to a delay of nearly 20 minutes due to crowd disturbances. Bedfordshire Police officers Colin Cooke and Phil Evans were among the 40 police officers injured, with Cooke being knocked unconscious by a slab of concrete. Evans eventually resuscitated Cooke, who had stopped breathing entirely, under a fusillade of attacks himself. Following the tie, nuts, bolts, glass bottles and even a knife were found in the goalmouth in front of Millwall's support. Of the 31 hooligans hauled before the courts as a result of the violence, a number identified themselves as supporters of West Ham in an attempt to fool the courts and the media. By this stage, Millwall's reputation was in tatters. Millwall's next away game, against Brentford, was postponed on police advice, being played out months later at the end of the season on a Sunday.

Two months later, before kick-off at the 1985 European Cup final between Liverpool and Juventus at Heysel Stadium in Brussels, Belgium, 39 Juventus fans died after a wall collapsed at the crumbling stadium. The Liverpool supporters were blamed for the disaster, leading to English clubs being banned from European competition by UEFA for the next five years. West Ham missed out on a UEFA Cup place as a result of finishing third in 1986, their record league finish to date.

As a result of the ban, supporters of English clubs took to pre-season friendlies in order to get their continental fix. Around 1am on 8 August 1986, onboard the *Koningin Beatrix* ferry from Harwich to the Netherlands, where Manchester United and West Ham United were both on tour to play Ajax and Den Haag respectively, around 100 Manchester United and thirty West Ham fans clashed whilst the 30,000-ton ferry was en route to the Hoek van Holland ferry terminal across the North Sea. A 21-year-old Manchester United supporter was admitted to hospital with head injuries and stab wounds in a brawl that saw three others stabbed. Upon turning around back to Harwich, fourteen people were arrested. Ferries and West Ham in the '80s wasn't a good mix. In 1989, en route to a World Cup qualification game between Sweden and England, West Ham fans were "dealing in drugs on a large scale" on a trip that saw 24-year-old England fan, Robert Ayling from Plymouth, fall overboard.

Although the events mentioned so far during the 1980s may seem insignificant to the general overview of Millwall and West Ham, it's important to understand the decaying state of football during the '80s, so much so that Prime Minister Margaret Thatcher so was getting involved, pushing for ID cards to be carried at Football League grounds.

By the mid-1980s, Thatcher and the establishment were thoroughly sick of football and all the perceived ills surrounding the sport. In May 1985, the Heysel Stadium disaster (killing 39 people), the Bradford City fire (killing

56 people), a riot between Birmingham City and Leeds United (killing 15-year-old Leeds supporter Ian Hambridge) and the previously mentioned events forced Thatcher's hand and action was finally implemented against not just football hooligans, but football in general. In 1985, a member of Chelsea's Headhunters firm, Kevin Whitton, was sentenced to life imprisonment for assault after brutally attacking American citizens in a pub on the King's Road in Chelsea. Although his sentence was later reduced three years on appeal, it was clear to see that the government wasn't taking the situation lightly. In January 1986, dawn raids were conducted across the south of England, primarily targeting members of Millwall's Bushwackers and West Ham's Inter City Firm after the riots at Luton and on the *Koningin Beatrix* ferry respectively as part of Operation Full Time. Multiple policing operations would follow in the next few years, aimed at rooting out hooliganism in the game.

On the evening of 4 October 1986, ten years on from the untimely death of Ian Pratt, mindless criminality once again dominated newspaper columns. That afternoon, Millwall had lost 2-1 away to South London rivals Crystal Palace, sending Palace to the top of the Second Division and Millwall into the relegation places. Millwall supporter John Johnstone and his friends travelled to Central London from Selhurst Park following the game, causing trouble on the city's public transportation system along the way – Johnstone attacked a passenger and a ticket inspector with his fists. Upon arriving at Charing Cross station, after being alerted by the train driver, the British Transport Police briefly held Johnstone and co. before allowing the group of six to continue with their evening. Johnstone and his group were almost immediately involved in another confrontation a minute down The Strand at a McDonald's, pulling a knife on a patron. Their thirst for violence was still not quenched, setting upon passers-by at Trafalgar Square and Charing Cross station. Terry Burns, a 19-year-old West Ham supporting labourer from Maidstone, was on a night out in London's West End, before retreating to Charing Cross after a fight broke out at a Covent Garden pub. Burns and his friends were spotted by Johnstone and his group, who asked Burns who he supported, to which Burns replied truthfully. The realisation of finding a football supporter, who supported Millwall's fiercest rivals, was like a drug to Johnstone and his gang, who bolted after Burns, chasing him out of Embankment station, howling death threats and shouts of "Millwall" at him, before stabbing his friend in the neck and arm with the very knife that Johnstone had proudly flaunted hours earlier in McDonald's. Burns met a dead-end down Villiers Street, being cornered moments later by the Millwall supporting gang. Burns was pounced upon, being stabbed six times, each stab wound puncturing his vital organs. The gang subsequently retreated back into South London via Hungerford Bridge. Just over a year later, Johnstone and Trevor Dunn, both 21-years-old and from Lewisham, were acquitted of Burns' murder at the Old Bailey, due to a lack of evidence, with no witnesses for the fatal stabbings.

In the aftermath of the fatal stabbing, a grim scoreboard was drawn up on a documentary about the British Transport Police, claiming the score between Millwall and West Ham as 1-1, in reference to Pratt and Burns' deaths.

With all the unsavoury scenes surrounding the pair in the '80s, it's easy to forget football was still being played. As a result of English clubs being handed a ban due to the events at Heysel in 1985, the idea of the Full Members' Cup was conceived, open to every team in the top two tiers of English football. Interest in the cup, initially sponsored by Simod, an obscure Italian shoe manufacturer, was poor. Less than half of the 44 eligible teams entered the first edition of the cup, with Charlton Athletic recording a then-record low attendance of 817 at home against Bradford City at their temporary home of Selhurst Park the following year. Clearly a popular tournament, then. With another domestic English competition up for grabs, the chances of Millwall and West Ham facing each other slightly increased. As if by magic, the two clubs were paired against each other, to play on 10 November 1987 at Upton Park. The events of the past decade-and-a-half had set the bad blood in motion for the tie, with over three times the normal police presence on duty for the Tuesday night cup tie in East London. Despite West Ham taking the lead through academy product Alan Dickens just over ten minutes into the second half, the Lions fought back, scoring twice in a two-minute salvo, thanks to goals from Tony Cascarino and Teddy Sheringham. Cleverly, the Millwall duo chose to keep their celebrations muted in front of the away end, which being heavily watched by a line of police officers. Out of the 11,337 in attendance, which was West Ham's lowest home gate all season, forty people were arrested on a night that saw two police helicopters patrol the East London sky.

Millwall's win, the first over the Hammers at Upton Park since the pair were elected to the Football League, was the second in a six-game win streak in all competitions, with Cascarino netting eight times during the run. Something special was stirring down at The Den. Such runs for Millwall were uncommon. Starting in February and ending in May, Millwall embarked on another unbeaten run, winning seven games consecutively in a twelve-game unbeaten streak. The final game of Millwall's run came away at Hull City on 2 May 1988. Ireland international Kevin O'Callaghan netted an eleventh-minute penalty for Millwall in front of an estimated Lions following of 6,000 – which, if correct, would account for well over half of the 10,036 gate at Boothferry Park. In the most un-Millwall style, the Lions did it the easy way. No scares, no worries, no repeats of the 'promotion' fiasco in 1972. Millwall were a First Division time for the first time in their history. With their promotion, Millwall became the final professional London club to play in the top tier, with Cascarino and Sheringham netting 23 and 24 goals respectively, accounting for 58% of Millwall's tally during the 1987-88 season. Maybe in more traditional Millwall fashion, the club lost 4-1 at home against Blackburn Rovers on the final day of the season. That didn't matter though, Millwall had achieved what many of their fans thought was the impossible – First Division football.

Off the pitch, Millwall were also making a conceited effort to clean up their reputation, which had taken perhaps it's heaviest battering following the distasteful scenes at Luton in 1985. During their promotion season, Millwall were voted community club of the year, thanks in no small part to becoming the first English club to open a crèche, situated at nearby Monson Primary School.

Millwall, who had managed to retain the services of Cascarino and Sheringham, took to the First Division like a duck to water, staying unbeaten for the first ten games in all competitions in the 1988-89 season, with Millwall's front two scoring fourteen between them. Prior to Millwall and West Ham's first ever top flight meeting on 3 December 1988, the Lions had only lost one league game, coming away to Middlesbrough at the end of October. On the flip side, West Ham were struggling at the wrong end of the table, having played fourteen games, winning just twice, drawing three times and losing nine until the game at The Den. As Hammers fans, a number of whom were walking wounded after clashes in the streets before kick-off, made their way to the away end at The Den, they were greeted with sinister graffiti sprayed on the turnstiles urging the travelling West Ham supporters to retreat or "die". Millwall came into the game as favourites, in front of 20,105 spectators, Millwall's biggest attendance for twelve years. Despite the big gate, the game was somewhat of an anti-climax as a heavy police presence focused on the terraces. The only goal of the game came after Millwall left-back Ian Dawes attempted a back pass to goalkeeper Brian Horne – the onrushing Alan Dicks latched onto the ball a fraction of a second before Horne and the ball kindly fell to fellow West Ham academy graduate Paul Ince, who had the easy task of slotting the ball into an open goal in front of Millwall's support on 18 minutes. As the game petered out, with Millwall's hopes of securing a result slipping away, chants of "you'll never make the station" flared up from the home support. At full-time, coins and other projectiles rained down on the Hammers players as they made their way down the tunnel, down into the bowels of The Den. Crowd disorder was kept to a minimum during the game, however, clashes broke out in the streets in New Cross following the game. The win marked West Ham's 1,000[th] win in the Football League; a rare bright spark for the Hammers in the 88-89 season – the club failed to pick up another win for over a month following the win against their bitter rivals.

Alarm bells for the Hammers' survival hopes were already ringing in December '88 and by April 1989, desperation had set in. With seven games left of the season remaining, Millwall, backed by a healthy contingent of away fans, made their way across to East London. Basked in sunshine, the tie was shrouded in controversy from the very start, after a section of the away support refused to observe a minute's silence for the Hillsborough disaster that occurred a week prior leaving 95 dead (at the time of kick-off; the figure later rose to 97 in July 2021, following the death of Andrew Devine). West Ham arguably enjoyed their best league performance of the season. Cult hero Julian Dicks opened the scoring with a long-range strike that squirmed through the arms of Millwall 'keeper Horne.

Two minutes later, Dickens added a second, with George Parris scoring in front of the South Bank just before the half-time whistle to send the Hammers into the break 3-0 up. With no more goals to report, West Ham had completed the first 'double' in the derby since the pair had been elected to the Football League. As usual, twenty were arrested in scuffles outside Upton Park before and after the game, with an axe being confiscated.

Despite the win, West Ham remained marooned at the bottom of the table on 26 points, ten points off safety, whilst Millwall were flying high in 7th place. Notwithstanding their best efforts, including winning four of their last six games, West Ham were eventually relegated in 19th place on 38 points, two points off safety, with manager John Lyall departing the club at the end of the season after 34 years of service to West Ham as a youth team player, first team player, youth team manager and first team manager. After their collapse at Upton Park, Millwall failed to win another game for the rest of the campaign, conceding eleven goals in their final four games of the season – a big slump after a promising start.

Millwall's poor form would extend into the following season. Despite another promising start, topping the First Division in September 1989, Millwall would go onto win just two more league games all season, failing to win an away game in the league all season. After slipping into a perilous position over the Christmas period, Millwall manager John Docherty called upon Paul Goddard, affectionately christened Sarge due to his Boys' Brigade connections, to try and claw the Lions out of trouble. Moving from Derby County in December 1989 for a fee of £800,000, Goddard was the subject of Millwall's record transfer outlay, only eclipsed in January 2019 when Tom Bradshaw's loan move from Barnsley was made into a permanent deal. Goddard, who signed for West Ham in 1980, wasn't received well in South London due to his West Ham connections, for whom he scored 71 times in 213 appearances in all competitions for. The forward was regarded as a "waste of money" after failing to have any real impact on Millwall's survival hopes – a feeling that still lingers in the minds of Millwall's support from a certain generation, even today. Goddard himself recalls that his shirt was ripped from his own back on his debut at The Den against Derby on New Year's Day 1990. 'Sarge' eventually left for Ipswich

Town in early 1991. In a twist of fate, Goddard came off the bench for his Ipswich debut at home to Millwall.

Millwall were eventually relegated without a fight. The Lions' last win of the season came in an FA Cup third round replay at home against Manchester City on 15 January 1990, with Goddard and Sheringham scoring in a 3-1 win. Their last league win stretched back even further to mid-December, beating Aston Villa 2-0 at home. A streak of eighteen games without tasting victory condemned the toothless Lions to relegation, finishing rock bottom on 26 points, 17 points off former antagonists Luton in 17th place. Millwall's return to the second tier would be without Tony Cascarino, who, with relegation looming, left in March 1990 for Aston Villa for a fee of £1.1 million.

Chapter 7:
All Change In The 1990s

The 1990s rolled around with renewed hope for football. It finally looked as if the war was being won against hooliganism. Several undercover policing operations set up during the second half of the 1980s, such as Operation Own Goal beginning in 1985, designed to infiltrate Chelsea's Headhunters firm, secured the convictions of football hooligans across the country. The increased installation and use of closed-circuit television systems in British football grounds presented another challenge for 'weekend offenders' to get away scot-free. Another nail in the coffin for hooliganism was the emergence of the rave scene. A new music genre named acid house had migrated across the Atlantic to the United Kingdom in the late '80s, along with ecstasy. The effects of ecstasy make users feel loved up – a big difference from the violence seen during the '80s. LSD also made a comeback, which didn't please everybody – the Headhunters took to producing a shirt with "Hooligans Against Acid" emblazoned on the front.

The tragic events at Bradford City and Hillsborough changed football forever in England, with all-seater stadiums becoming the norm due to the recommendations put forward by Popplewell and Taylor's reports respectively. As a consequence of the Taylor Report, all clubs competing in the top two tiers of English football were required to have all-seater stadia.

With both teams back in the Second Division for the 1990-91 season, the first meeting between the pair in the new decade was on the horizon. On 10 November 1990, the pair met at The Den, with Millwall sitting fifth in the Second Division, three places behind West Ham in second. Two days prior, One Canada Square in Canary Wharf was topped off, signifying a massive change on the Isle of Dogs and East London in general in the eighty years since Millwall vacated the island. The project, changing the area from dockland poverty to a glittering financial district, was labelled by soon-to-be-ousted Prime Minister Margaret Thatcher as the "most exciting that we had ever known". An all-ticket affair, the only game that week in the entirety of Britain to be all-ticket, kicked off 15 minutes late due to clashes involving an estimated 4,000 fans outside The Den, with cars being damaged in the crossfire. After an eventful first 45 minutes that ultimately saw no goals, Millwall midfielder Paul Stephenson fired the Lions into the lead two minutes into the second half, with an 18-yard volley giving goalkeeper Luděk Mikloško no chance in the West Ham goal. Exactly three years after their last win against the Hammers, in the Full Members' Cup, it looked as if Millwall were heading for their first league win against their rivals in eleven years, before Frank McAvennie levelled proceedings, converting a cross from point-blank range in front of Millwall's support, prompting fury. Described as the first violent clash between football fans in the 1990-91 season, three people were hospitalised in what was recounted as "full-scale rioting". The gate of 20,591 was Millwall's biggest home attendance by far during the 90-91 season, with the tie attracting an increase of nearly 13,000 from the Lions' fixture against Oxford United three days prior.

Four months later, the two, both fighting for promotion

back into the First Division, met again. For the clash at Upton Park, the authorities were taking no risks. Millwall's away ticket allocation was cut to 2,300 with the game kicking off at midday on a Sunday on police advice. Chelsea's League Cup semi-final clash with Sheffield Wednesday at Stamford Bridge also kicked off at the same time to prevent clashes between Chelsea, Millwall and West Ham on the District Line. Coming into the tie as table toppers, the onus was on West Ham to take the game to their rivals from South London. After a spell of early pressure, Ian Bishop's pinpoint cross was met by the head of McAvennie, who duly converted from twelve yards out. On the stroke of half-time, Millwall got back into the tie. Summer signing Jon Goodman took advantage of Tim Breacker's poor touches in the West Ham area, side-footing a first time effort past Mikloško. Out for the second 45 minutes of play, it was West Ham's turn to take advantage of Millwall errors three minutes into the half, with McAvennie pouncing upon Brian Horne's failure to properly claim the ball, subsequently passing the ball into an empty Millwall net. The following week, Horne was dropped in favour of Keith Branagan for a run of thirteen games. On the hour mark, the Hammers doubled their lead, with goalscorer turning provider –

McAvennie's cross met the head of Trevor Morley. West Ham ended the day top of the Second Division, with a four-point gap over nearest challengers Oldham Athletic.

In typical West Ham soap opera fashion, drama wasn't far around the corner after the fixture, however, for once, it didn't involve Millwall. The following month, Morley was allegedly stabbed by his Norwegian wife, Hege. Rumours of Morley's infidelity were quickly twisted by the press, with wild rumours, conjured up by Fleet Street, quickly being contorted into terrace taunts. Although the speculation was unfounded, the bizarre start to West Ham's spring somehow didn't derail West Ham's promotion hopes. In Billy Bonds' first full season in charge of West Ham, with Morley returning to action in April, the Hammers won promotion back to the First Division, finishing runners-up to Oldham Athletic. Despite the 46-game season coming to an end, Millwall were still in the promotion hunt, finishing fifth, qualifying for the play-offs in the process. Millwall's play-off campaign was short-lived and a disaster. The Lions were humbled 4-1 at the Goldstone Ground against sixth placed Brighton & Hove Albion, after initially taking the lead through Paul Stephenson. In an all or nothing second leg at The Den, a glimmer of hope appeared in the South London sky after loanee John McGinlay opened the scoring for the Lions before two second half goals for Brighton ended Millwall's promotion hopes. The game marked Teddy Sheringham's final game for the club, moving to Nigel Clough's Nottingham Forest for a fee of £2 million after an ever-present season in which he made 55 appearances in all competitions, scoring an impressive 38 times. Sheringham would later sign for West Ham, playing for the club 87 times during the mid-2000s.

In order to plug the Sheringham-sized hole, Millwall acquired the services of former Tottenham Hotspur frontman Mark Falco ahead of the 1991-92 season, but things weren't the same without Cascarino or Sheringham. Millwall finished in 15th place, in a much-changed squad. West Ham, on the other hand, weren't faring much better. The Hammers' stint back in the top flight of English football didn't go as planned, being relegated straight back into the second tier, finishing rock bottom in the process. West Ham's disastrous season was probably summed up best by non-league side Farnborough Town taking the Hammers to a replay in the third round of the FA Cup.

Another change for English football was on the horizon. As part of the 'clean up' of English football, the Premier League was founded. Talk of the elite clubs in the country forming a breakaway league had been on the cards for a number of years, with a massive new television deal bringing money into English football that had never been seen before. As a result of Millwall's sub-par season and West Ham's relegation the previous season, the distinction of playing in the inaugural Premier League season passed both clubs by.

With both clubs back in the second tier (now renamed the First Division as part of the restructure), it was time for the duo to face off yet again. Both clubs had been enjoying a decent start to the 1992-93 season, looking to gain promotion to the newly formed Premier League. Played at noon on a Sunday, once again on police advice, Millwall took advantage of West Ham's fatigue following their Anglo-Italian Cup adventures in the northern Italian city of Cremona four days prior. Five minutes before the half-time whistle, West Ham midfielder Mark Robson was adjudged to have fouled Millwall's Alex Rae, who had been causing the Hammers defence problems all game, in the penalty area. Welsh international Malcolm Allen proceeded to fire his spot kick into the roof of the net, in front of West Ham's travelling support. Phil Barber doubled Millwall's lead on 55 minutes, before Robson redeemed himself with a mazy run through the Lions' defence, with thirteen minutes remaining. Millwall managed to see the game out on an overcast mid-November afternoon, beating the Hammers for the first time in five years. In reality, there was more action on the pitch than between the fans, with six players picking up bookings in a twenty-minute period in the first half.

Some things transcend even the fiercest of rivalries, though. Bobby Moore needs no introduction. The man who captained both England and West Ham United to international and European glory was not only revered in the East End, but in every city, town, village and home in the country. Moore had been suffering with health problems during the early '90s, undergoing an operation for colon cancer. Never one to seek the limelight, Moore announced he was suffering from cancer on 14 February 1993, late into his treatment. Ten days later, unexpectedly, Moore passed away, becoming the first member of England's 1966 World Cup winning squad to die. A plethora of supporters from different clubs added the tributes to the gates at the Boleyn Ground, with Millwall scarves and shirts being there for everybody to see in very healthy numbers. To this day, Millwall Football Club themselves are still big supporters of the Bobby Moore Fund for Cancer Research UK, along with West Ham.

In the five-month gap since the duo's last meeting, the promotion race to the Premier League was heating up. In the seventeen league games the Hammers had contested since Christmas Day, Billy Bonds' men had only lost twice, both by one goal margins. Millwall had also been keeping up with the promotion pace, beating Brentford and Peterborough United 6-1 and 4-0 respectively at home during January in the space of ten days. Keen to cut the gap with their rivals, the Lions romped into an early lead, with summer signing Jamie Moralee waltzing past Steve Potts in the West Ham defence, finishing a one-on-one in the opening minute to send the away end into utter pandemonium. If any spell of football summed up the hectic nature of the rivalry, the opening 15 minutes on 28 March 1993 in East London fit like a glove. Thirteen minutes into the tie, West Ham equalised, after a David Speedie overhead kick found the boot of Kevin Keen, who converted. Think of Marco van Basten's volley in the Euro 1988 final (from a slightly more favourable angle) and you're there. A minute later, West Ham edged in front, thanks to a more conventional finish from Trevor Morley. Within the space of two minutes, Millwall had gone from winning to losing. With just over ten minutes remaining, Millwall stalwart Keith Stevens, who would go onto make 546 appearances for the club, levelled the scores at 2-2 with a looping header. The second placed Hammers had ample opportunities to cut Newcastle United's lead at the top of the table to three points, however, Millwall's defence remained resolute, clearing an effort from Morley off the line. Speedie spurned two late chances, much to the delight of Millwall's travelling support. West Ham finished the Sunday in second place, with the Lions sat fourth.

Coming to the business end of the 1992-93 season, with both clubs vying for promotion to the Premier League for the first time, Millwall won just once more following the clash at Upton Park, a 1-0 home win against fellow South Londoners Charlton. In East London, West Ham won six games out of their remaining eight, winning promotion into the Premier League, after a comprehensive 2-0 against Cambridge United, sparking jubilant scenes. Millwall ended the campaign in seventh place, one place and six points off the play-off places.

The 1990s were a period of all change. Millwall's success during the late '80s saw their average attendance grow from 4,010 in the 1982-83 season to 15,468 in their first season in the top flight in 1988-89. Following the publication of the Taylor Report in 1990, pressure was on Millwall to move home. Stepping into the '90s, The Den was now looking more outdated by the year. By 1993, the ban on English clubs competing in Europe had finished, the First Division had morphed into the Premier League, the European Cup had transformed into the UEFA Champions League and the expansive terraces, perimeter fences and decaying stands at The Den were no longer fashionable or fit for use in football's new era. In January 1989, whispers of Millwall moving home first cropped up, with a site at Senegal Fields, a stones throw away from South Bermondsey station, being the preferred option. Rumours of moving back to the Isle of Dogs were abound, with new developments on the island cropping up seemingly every day, however, Millwall's board and Lewisham Council were desperate to keep Millwall in

South London. Construction at the Senegal Fields site began in 1992, with Millwall's shiny new all-seater stadium, also called The Den, being built in just 57 weeks. The stadium was the first professional stadium built in the country to be compliant with the recommendations of the Taylor Report.

The gates at The (soon to be old) Den were closed forever on 8 May 1993. A 3-0 loss against Bristol Rovers in front of a crowd of 15,821 wasn't the best way to depart The Den. A final pitch invasion, in completely good nature, signed off Millwall's time at their home of 93 years. Animosity in sections of Millwall's fanbase was high as a result of the move, with a homemade banner denouncing club chairman Reg Burr of murdering The Den being seen on the pitch on the stadium's final day.

Old habits die hard, though. After another impressive season in the newly renamed First Division, Millwall finished third, once again qualifying for the play-offs. After losing 2-0 away to Derby County in the first leg, pressure was on Millwall to get off to a good start in the second leg. Three first half goals from Derby crushed Millwall hopes of top tier football for another season. In frustration at the scoreline, which was still 2-0 to Derby at the time, the tie was temporarily delayed following a number of home supporters invading the pitch, whilst scuffles between Millwall fans and the police broke out. Before the full-time whistle, which was blown two minutes early, another pitch invasion took place that saw Derby goalkeeper Martin Taylor attacked. Following the heated game, a BBC Radio Derby broadcasting van was overturned with several parked cars also coming under attack. Derby manager Roy McFarland added further scorn towards the Lions, claiming Derby duo Paul Williams and Gary Charles had been on the receiving end of racial abuse that May night.

Just over a year later, the Millwall support at their new home were in hot water again, after Sheffield Wednesday's number one Kevin Pressman was confronted by a Millwall fan during a League Cup tie, who allegedly blasted a death threat towards him, before being escorted away by police. The incident came just months after a spanner was lobbed towards Reading goalkeeper Simon Sheppard at Elm Park during a 2-1 Millwall victory in August 1995, earning Millwall the nickname of "the spanners", typically used by Charlton fans. From October 1920, when Newport goalkeeper John Cooper was knocked out by a member of Millwall's support, resulting in The Den's first closure, to the League Cup incident in October 1995, being a goalkeeper against Millwall had always been risky business. Curiously, Pressman would later join Millwall as a goalkeeping coach, staying at the club for six years between 2012 and 2018.

After their flirtation with aspirations of regaining their top tier status during the early 1990s, the Lions were relegated on the final day of the 1995-96 season. Millwall enjoyed a stellar start to the season, sitting top of the table in December 1995. Looking to regain form after a run of three consecutive defeats, Mick McCarthy's side travelled to the north east to face second placed Sunderland in a game that was already being considered as a defining game in the race for promotion. Sunderland ran riot, dispatching Millwall with ease, putting six goals past the Lions without reply. After a 2-0 defeat at the hands of Southend United on 3 February 1996, McCarthy resigned, being appointed manager of the Republic of Ireland two days later. At the time of McCarthy's departure, Millwall were fourteen points off the drop. The incoming Jimmy Nicholl could not arrest Millwall's poor form, winning just four of Millwall's next sixteen games. Millwall's survival hopes all came down to Nicholl's seventeenth game in charge, away to play-off chasing Ipswich Town on the final day of the season. A 0-0 draw wasn't enough to secure Millwall's First Division status, with Portsmouth picking up all three points away to Huddersfield Town to survive the drop and consign Millwall to relegation.

Millwall started the following season strongly in the third tier, topping the table in early December 1996, before embarking on a run that saw just five league victories. A repeat of the previous season was avoided, with the Lions finishing 14th; however, hearts would've been in mouths at The Den as supporters saw their team plummet down the league table for the second consecutive season.

In May 1997, West Ham legend Billy Bonds was appointed as Millwall manager. After joining West Ham from Charlton at the age of twenty, Bonds racked up 799 appearances and 61 goals for West Ham across 21 seasons in all competitions, to become West Ham's all-time record appearance holder. Following his playing career, Bonds was appointed as West Ham manager in February

1990, after the departure of Lou Macari in controversial circumstances. Bonds managed a total of 227 games over a four-year spell at West Ham, after working his way up from a coaching role, following his retirement in 1988. Bonds, who was coaching at Reading at the time of his appointment, was chosen for the Millwall job over former West Ham and Millwall forward Clive Allen and Brighton & Hove Albion manager Steve Gritt, who would later join the Lions as reserve team manager, becoming caretaker manager for a spell in 2000. Upon his appointment, Bonds, who was born south of the Thames in Woolwich, attempted to quell any ill-feeling regarding his appointment, pointing to his South London roots and confessing he had numerous family members who supported Millwall. On 7 May 1994, 364 days after his appointment, Bonds was sacked by Millwall chairman Theo Paphitis after a disappointing 18th placed finish in the third tier of English football, with Millwall embarking on their traditional end of season car crash, failing to win any of their final eight games. Bonds was replaced by Millwall legend Keith Stevens in a player-manager role, alongside defender Alan McLeary. Both aged 33, they became the sixth managerial change at the club in the past two years, beating Brentford manager Micky Adams,

Northampton Town's Ian Atkins and former Scottish international Joe Jordan to the post.

Millwall end
their ties with Bonds

T he Second Division strugglers Millwall have parted company with their manager Billy Bonds.

Millwall's chairman Theo Paphitis said yesterday that Bonds's experience at a higher level with West Ham was not appropriate for Millwall's modest standing. They ended the season three places above the relegation zone.

The Guardian, page 68, 8 May 1998

Bonds' departure from West Ham four years prior in 1994 came in more acrimonious circumstances. Bonds was effectively replaced by former teammate Harry Redknapp, who served as his assistant after a spell managing on the south coast at AFC Bournemouth. 'Bonzo', as he was nicknamed by the West Ham support, rejected a chance to move upstairs, with Redknapp becoming the main man at West Ham. Bonds' 27-year association with West Ham was over, with Redknapp being the man to lead the club in the 21st century.

Chapter 8:
Stepping Into The 21st Century

More change was on the horizon in the new millennium. The 1990s changed football in the United Kingdom forever – and, arguably, for the better. The game switched from being regarded as an unsafe environment to bring children to, to a safe, sanitised and family friendly affair. Euro 96, alongside the Cool Britannia youth culture that had engulfed the country in the mid-'90s, once again made football cool and trendy; almost a miracle from football leaping from disaster after disaster in the second half of the 1980s.

It looked as if the dark days in regards to football violence were behind us at this stage. So much so, that hooliganism was now being romanticised in the form of films, with *Green Street* (2005) and *The Firm* (2009) both being based on Millwall and West Ham's rivalry. Being released less than a month after the disorder at a League Cup game between the two (much, much more on this later), *The Firm* picked up more traction than originally bargained for, after Scotland Yard used stills from the film by mistake, in wanted pictures issued after the violence. Vertigo Films, the production company behind the film, stated they were "delighted" with Scotland Yard issuing the photos and the subsequent media attention.

On the pitch, Millwall and West Ham started off the new millennium in contrasting fashions. Millwall were still in the Second Division, still feeling the effects from Nicholl's reign at the club.

Rivals West Ham saw the new millennium in a much healthier fashion. The Academy of Football was reaping rewards, producing future England internationals such as Michael Carrick, Joe Cole, Rio Ferdinand and Frank Lampard, the latter three of whom helped West Ham finish fifth in the 1998-99 Premier League, qualifying for the Intertoto Cup as a result. Carrick made his debut for the club in the competition, playing the last ten minutes in the second leg tie against Finnish outfit FC Jokerit. The Hammers ended up winning the competition, qualifying for the UEFA Cup as a result, meaning the club fought in five different competitions during the 1999-2000 season.

In September 2000, Millwall appointed former Scotland international Mark McGhee, following the departure of Stevens and McLeary. In McGhee's first season at the club, Millwall gained promotion back into Division One, with club legend Neil Harris scoring 27 league goals en route to the league title, helping the club secure a record 93 points.

The following season, Millwall were aiming for another promotion, aiming to regain top tier status for the first time since 1990. As the confetti settled on their record-breaking promotion season, Harris was diagnosed with testicular cancer, undergoing surgery as a result. Harris' temporary withdrawal from the side was plugged by the goals of Tim Cahill, Steve Claridge and Richie Sadlier, scoring 48 goals between them in all competitions. Harris, who made a return to the side in December, helped push Millwall over the play-off line, scoring twice in a 3-1 win against Grimsby Town to set up a play-off meeting with Birmingham City.

After a 1-1 draw up in Birmingham at St Andrew's, all eyes were on The Den to see who would face Norwich City in the play-off final at the Millennium Stadium in Cardiff. After a scrappy game of missed opportunities, Stern John, who had joined Birmingham a few months prior, turned home a square ball from Steve Vickers in the 90th minute to send Birmingham to Cardiff. Birmingham's triumph was like a red rag to a bull. After minor pitch excursions following the full-time whistle that required the use of police horses to disperse a handful of Millwall fans, around 900 Millwall supporters rampaged in the streets of Bermondsey, incensed at Millwall's failure to reach the play-off final. 47 police officers and 26 police horses were injured in scenes that saw petrol bombs used, bricks hurled and cars set alight in the surrounding South London streets. Officers on duty that night likened the events to the Bosnian War and the worst hooliganism seen on English shores since the '80s. The Metropolitan Police considered suing Millwall over the violence, however were dissuaded after the club made a donation to a charity dedicated to helping injured police officers. Birmingham ended up winning promotion to the Premier League, beating Norwich on penalties after a 1-1 draw after extra time.

As a result of the disorder against Birmingham and generally across the 2001-02 season, away fans were banned, home and away, for games against Burnley, Leicester City, Nottingham Forest, Stoke City and Wolverhampton Wanderers.

The following season, neither Millwall nor West Ham started the season off well, with West Ham sitting bottom after eight games under the management of Glenn Roeder, who had replaced Redknapp the previous summer. On 17 October 2002, young full-back Glen Johnson – who would later go onto make 54 appearances for England – was loaned to Millwall on an initial one-month loan deal. Despite Roeder acknowledging the rivalry, he labelled Millwall's coaching staff as "excellent" and the move would be ideal to give Johnson experience in senior men's football. Almost to be expected, Johnson's loan move was met with discontent in sections of both fanbases. Johnson made eight appearances during his time south of the river and his time at the Lions helped the defender break into West Ham's squad for the rest of their ill-fated 02-03 season. At the business end of the season, Roeder suffered a brain tumour and was replaced by Hammers legend Sir Trevor

Brooking. Despite Brooking's best efforts, that included recalling the exiled Paolo di Canio to the side and picking up two wins from the final three games of the season, West Ham were relegated back into the First Division, competing in the league for the first time in ten years. Johnson, and prodigy Joe Cole, left West Ham for cross-city rivals Chelsea for a combined fee of £12.6 million. The pair, alongside former West Ham academy graduate Frank Lampard, would later pick up League Cup and Premier League medals with the club the following season.

As a result of West Ham's relegation, rivalries were reignited for the 2003-04 season. With no First Division rivalries to speak of (maybe with the exception of Ipswich Town and Norwich City playing each other), all eyes were on when Millwall and West Ham would be scheduled to face each other for the first time in ten years. There wasn't a long wait. The fixture computer paired the two to face off against each other on the last weekend in September 2003, a fixture quickly changed to a noon kick-off on police advice. Five days before the showdown, on 23 September 2003, West Ham first had to navigate a League Cup tie away to Cardiff City.

Jermain Defoe, who had attracted controversy after requesting a transfer away from the club less than 24 hours after West Ham's relegation, netted a hat-trick in a 3-2 comeback win for the Hammers. As a dress rehearsal for the visit of Millwall on the Sunday, 200 West Ham 'hooligans' made their way down to the Welsh capital, engaging in disorder that saw a number of arrests on both sides, including footballer Craig Hughes, who would later lead the line for Newport County.

An alcohol ban was in place for the 31,626 inside Upton Park on the Sunday. Such was the anticipation for the tie, and also to prevent fans travelling to West Ham looking for trouble, Millwall organised a beam-back at The Den for those who weren't lucky enough to be part of the 2,543 strong away end in East London. West Ham implemented a scheme where supporters needed membership or a prior booking history in order to purchase tickets, albeit only after a number of Millwall supporters had purchased tickets in the home end. Being the first real derby between the two in the internet era, bravado and threats were noted on messageboards of supporters of both clubs. These threats largely didn't come to fruition, with 800 extra Met Police officers helping keep the peace as much as can be kept in a game between Millwall and West Ham. With no trouble inside the ground, a few small-scale clashes in the streets of East Ham and Plaistow were quickly quelled. The police were on their game, with a large group of Millwall supporters being spotted and picked up by the force in North Woolwich. It's easy to forget that a football match is actually the reason behind all of this. Irish international David Connolly, who joined in the summer, opened the scoring on 23 minutes for the Hammers. With both teams fighting to make early headway for promotion, West Ham had the better opportunities in the first 45 minutes, with Defoe seeing a shot cleared off the line. Although Matthew Etherington, another summer signing, hit the post after the half-time break, the visitors came out for the second 45 reinvigorated, with winger Paul Ifill seeing an effort crash against the crossbar with twenty minutes remaining. Less than five minutes later, Millwall frontman Tim Cahill headed the Lions level, thanks to a pinpoint cross from Ifill. Cahill's equaliser sparked something in Millwall, with the Cahill and Ifill testing David James in the West Ham goal in search of a winner.

Defoe had a golden opportunity to win all three points for the Hammers, if only if he squared the ball to an unmarked and free Connolly. Defoe elected to try a shot and subsequently missed, not helping his reputation at all in East London. Perhaps the most surprising result of the day was there only being a single arrest.

Just over a month later, 93 West Ham supporters were arrested after an attack on The Cockerel pub down Tottenham High Road before a League Cup fourth round tie away to Spurs. The events seen during the early stages of the 2003-04 season showed hooliganism was still lurking, just not on the large scale seen a few decades prior.

In the succeeding months, both Millwall and West Ham were trotting along rather nicely in the First Division, with both clubs vying for a play-off spot. West Ham's automatic promotion hopes were severely hampered after an inconsistent winter period under new manager Alan Pardew, whilst Millwall were fighting on two fronts – the league and the FA Cup.

The second meeting between the two of the 2003-04 season was scheduled for 21 March 2004. Before the first showdown between the pair at The (New) Den, Millwall first had to overcome Second Division outfit Tranmere Rovers in an FA Cup quarter-final replay up north at Prenton Park. The Lions triumphed 2-1, thanks to early goals from Cahill and Harris, setting up a semi-final date with fellow First Division play-off chasers Sunderland at Villa Park.

After Millwall's midweek heroics, attention shifted to Bermondsey. No less than 1,118 police officers were on duty on the Sunday afternoon, the largest security presence English football has ever seen, costing a total of £270,000. Taking initiative from Millwall's move earlier in the season, West Ham showed the game live at Upton Park, with season ticket holders or members the only groups permitted to buy tickets in the away end. 16 minutes in, the Lions won a penalty, after West Ham winger Etherington fouled Paul Ifill in the 18-yard area. Neil Harris couldn't take advantage, seeing his spot kick saved by the legs of Stephen Bywater. Hammers defender Christian Dailly opened the scoring, expertly dispatching a cross into the far corner of the net. Unfortunately for

Dailly, and West Ham, it was Ifill's cross he converted, beating Bywater in the West Ham goal to put Millwall 1-0 up. Just 48 seconds into the second half, Cahill doubled Millwall's advantage with his head. Bywater got an arm to Cahill's effort, however, he was unable to repeat his penalty exploits. Three minutes later, Marlon Harewood halved the deficit from the penalty spot after Millwall defender Matt Lawrence handled inside the area. In a frantic start to the second half, Cahill broke away from Dailly, converting a bicycle kick unmarked from a corner to double his tally for the afternoon. Just past the hour mark, Bywater saw red after committing a professional foul on Harris, leading to a penalty. Bywater wasn't the only one to see red. West Ham supporters were enraged at their side crumbling before their very eyes and eight police horses and 50 police offers were hastily drafted in to contain the fans in the away end. Cahill buried his penalty into the Cold Blow Lane stand, missing the opportunity to grab his hat-trick and Millwall's fourth. The home side did get a fourth on 80 minutes, via loanee Nick Chadwick, blasting the white Mitre ball into the roof of the net, well out the reach of substitute goalkeeper Pavel Srníček. West Ham's embarrassment was compound and Millwall's joy was palpable, on a day that has gone down in the history of the rivalry as the Mother's Day Massacre, taking inspiration from the Saint Valentine's Day Massacre 75 years before. On Mother's Day 2004, Millwall's strike force were more deadly than Al Capone could have ever hoped to have been.

A poor finish to the league season saw Millwall finish tenth, whilst West Ham secured a play-off place, finishing fourth. Trips to Cardiff were on the cards for both sets of supporters in May 2004. Millwall had traversed their FA Cup semi-final, thanks to a first half volley from none other than Tim Cahill. Millwall had a free hit for the final, coming up against a star-studded Manchester United side, featuring the likes of Cristiano Ronaldo, Paul Scholes and Ruud van Nistelrooy. As widely expected, Millwall lost 3-0. Millwall's fans weren't the only set of supporters making their way back to London on the M4 from the Welsh capital in a despondent mood. After overcoming Ipswich in the semi-finals of the play-offs, a single Neil Shipperley goal for Crystal Palace was enough to send Palace into the Premier League at the expense of West Ham. Another season in the second tier, that was to be rebranded as

The Championship in the summer, for both sets of supporters.

As a result of their FA Cup exploits, Millwall embarked on their first ever European tour, being drawn against Hungarian league and cup double winners Ferencváros in the first round of the UEFA Cup. Despite being drawn against one of the heavyweights of Hungarian football, Millwall gave a good account of themselves in the first leg, taking the lead through the right foot of player-manager Dennis Wise, who converted from a direct free-kick 25 yards out from goal. Fradi, as they're commonly referred to back home, equalised through Péter Lipcsei twelve minutes from time, with a free-kick of his own. A 1-1 draw was a fair and credible result for Millwall in their first taste of European football. Things turned sour for the second leg. Millwall were defeated 3-1 at Fradi's Üllői úti Stadion, however, Millwall's exit wasn't what made headlines. Clashes raged in the streets of Budapest after an estimated 3,000 Millwall fans made the trip over to the Hungarian capital, despite only receiving a ticket allocation of 1,200. Two travelling Millwall supporters were left in serious conditions in hospital after being stabbed. Ferencváros, who hold somewhat of a reputation themselves, were later charged by UEFA after their fans threw missiles and shouted racist abuse at Millwall players.

Less than two months after Millwall's trip to Central Europe, West Ham made the short trip to South London on 21 November 2004. The near misses of the previous season in Cardiff whet Millwall's and West Ham's appetite for success, with promotion into the Premier League being the goal. The police were hoping for no near misses in regards to crowd disorder, implementing a policing operation costing a total of £600,000. With a reduced away allocation of 2,100, seeing the lower tier of the away end closed, coins and even a mobile phone rained down from the upper tier targeting Dennis Wise as Millwall won 1-0, thanks to a late Danny Dichio bullet header. Following the game, weapons, knives and ammonia in Jif lemon bottles (a tactic applied in years gone by) were found at Canning Town station. A group of Millwall fans also made the trip across to East London to attack a West Ham pub, despite the game being played at The Den.

With the 2004-05 season coming to a close, it was time for the pair to get reacquainted. With both sides hovering just outside of the play-off places, all eyes were on the pitch for once, in the knowledge that any result could skew the play-off and promotion pictures. Millwall started the Saturday afternoon (the first time a derby between the pair had been played on a Saturday in fifteen years) in ninth place, with West Ham sat one place above in eighth. Jamaica international Barry Hayles opened the scoring for the Lions in front of the Bobby Moore Stand at Upton Park, before Marlon Harewood levelled the scores ten minutes before half-time. The April 2005 meeting between the two would've come as a relief to the 1,000 police officers on duty. A 1-1 draw and no arrests being made – a landmark, being the first game between Millwall and West Ham in a number of years without anybody spending the night in the cells. As was to be expected, a few small-scale scuffles broke out before being quickly stopped by police. One senior policeman likened the post-match atmosphere as the final moments in the trenches in World War I before 'going over the top'.

The Hammers sneaked into the play-offs on the last day of the season, at the expense of Alan Pardew's former employers Reading. Before a ball was kicked in West Ham's highly anticipated ties with Ipswich, changes were in motion at The Den. Player-manager Dennis Wise tendered his resignation a day after the season's finale, following talks with new chairman Jeff Burnige, who himself resigned less than two months later. In an even more bizarre twist, Burnige's replacement for Wise, Steve Claridge, was sacked by Millwall 36 days into this tenure, having failed to even take charge of a competitive game. Turmoil at Millwall and joy for the Hammers, who regained their Premier League status at the Millennium Stadium – a Bobby Zamora finish being enough for West Ham to overcome Preston North End in Cardiff.

Just 348 days had passed before West Ham were back in Cardiff for another final, this time coming up against Champions League holders Liverpool. In what has been described as the best FA Cup final since the Matthews final in 1953, West Ham were in front twice, before a Steven Gerrard piledriver seconds into added time broke West Ham hearts. West Ham would go onto lose on penalties. Millwall fans also were left heartbroken in the spring of 2006, being relegated in a season which saw five managers occupy the home dugout at The Den (four if you discount Claridge's role).

Despite not facing each other in little over a year, the temptation for some Millwall and West Ham supporters to have a pop at each other was too great. On 10 June 2006, during a live showing of England's 1-0 group game victory over Paraguay in the World Cup, 100 rival Millwall and West Ham fans brawled in Canary Wharf's Canada Square, forcing the BBC, who had organised the screening, to pull the plug with ten minutes of the tie remaining, leaving over 3,000 peaceful spectators disappointed. Nothing much changes – 100 years on and the two clubs were still scrapping on the Isle of Dogs.

The next meeting between the pair could probably have a book of its own. On 12 August 2009, the draw for the second round of the League Cup was held. 36 balls had been pulled out of the pot, resulting in eighteen ties, none of which looked particularly interesting. With fourteen clubs waiting to see their ties, West Ham United were the next club to get pulled out, gaining the advantage of a home tie in the process. Thirteen clubs remaining. Millwall. A collective loss of composure in the upper echelons of the Met Police would have ensued. Contingency plans for the match, due to take place in thirteen days' time, were immediately drawn up. Millwall were entitled to an allocation of 15% of Upton Park's capacity under League Cup rulings, a total of 5,252 tickets, however, were only initially granted 1,500 tickets, much to Millwall's protestations, who cited the risk of ticketless fans making their way to East London. They would later be proven right, with ticketless fans roaming the streets and eventually gaining entry into the away end. West Ham later offered 800 more seats to Millwall, an offer that was hastily accepted. Twenty police horses and 750 officers, a significant drop from previous games between the pair, were on duty on the Tuesday evening. Hammers manager Gianfranco Zola, as mild mannered of a man you could hope to meet, quipped to the media that he wouldn't walk to the ground pre-match. Wise choice. Millwall supporters making the trip would be making a longer walk to the Boleyn Ground than usual, with trains not stopping at Upton Park station, meaning Millwall supporters would have to make the twenty-minute walk from East Ham station. Several District Line trains holding Millwall supporters were forcibly stopped at Upton Park station by their passengers on board. Said passengers flooded Green Street, embarking on the first of six hours of running street battles, beginning at Queen's Market. 125 extra officers were hastily drafted in after it was clear things were turning sour. The violence was pre-planned and organised according to the police, something that former ICF member Cass Pennant disputed in a column with *The Guardian*. Around fifteen minutes after kick-off, a Millwall supporter in his 40s was stabbed in the chest outside in Priory Road after becoming separated from the rest of his family. Small groups of West Ham supporters had been lurking in the estates behind the East Stand at Upton Park, weaving in and out of the blocks of flats, picking off Millwall supporters making their way to the away end, with another man suffering a laceration to the neck.

Around ten minutes after the stabbing, cult hero Neil Harris sent the away end into carnage, latching onto a long throw in, finishing from close range past a hapless Rob Green. Lions' midfielder Marc Laird nearly doubled Millwall's advantage, hitting the woodwork from range.

Millwall were heading for yet another famous victory over the Hammers, before West Ham academy product Junior Stanislas converted from the same spot Neil Harris did over an hour earlier. Scoring his first goal of the season, the 19-year-old's exuberant celebrations prompted a pitch invasion from all corners of the ground. Trouble had already been brewing in the corner between the West Stand and the Sir Trevor Brooking Stand, with a section of West Ham's support in the corner insistent on breaking through the lines of police and stewards and confronting Millwall's support.

Stanislas' late equaliser meant thirty more minutes of football was to be played. Thirty more minutes of ill-feeling. Thirty more minutes of provocation. Thirty more minutes of clashes. Eight minutes into extra-time, Millwall defender Andy Frampton was adjudged to have handled the ball inside the 18-yard area, allowing Stanislas the opportunity to convert from the penalty spot, putting West Ham in front for the first time on the night. Another knee slide celebration towards the home support meant another pitch invasion, this time forcing Millwall's players off the field of play. Another Academy of Football graduate, Zavon Hines, added some gloss to the scoreline, scoring a third, promoting another pitch invasion. The scenes were too much for Jack Collison, whose father passed away two days earlier on his way to West Ham's home tie against Tottenham. Collison bravely played the full 120 minutes. Bradley Allen, former footballer and brother to Clive Allen, stated he had never seen "such hatred" at a football game before. As well as the two knifing victims, over twenty injuries were reported, including a man with head injuries in Redclyffe Road, a stones throw away from Upton Park station.

The immediate enquiry into what went wrong was largely played out in the press. The following day, the *London Evening Standard* asked its readership if they believed West Ham should be expelled from the League Cup following the clashes. 73% of voters agreed West Ham's participation in the competition should come to an end, with just 27% believing West Ham should be allowed to stay in the competition. It wouldn't matter much, anyway. The following month, West Ham were the victims of a 3-1 win after extra-time away to Bolton Wanderers. Minister of Sport Gerry Sutcliffe tore apart West Ham, saying the scenes were a "disgrace to football", with Home Secretary Alan Johnson echoing Sutcliffe's words. The pair had a very real reason to condemn what happened. England were in the process of bidding for the 2018 World Cup and there was a very belief in the media the scenes at Upton Park could de-rail England's bid. The World Cup was eventually awarded to Russia – themselves no strangers to hooliganism.

Just over a month after the game, both Millwall and West Ham were slapped with FA charges, including violent behaviour, racism, encroaching on the field of play and the throwing of missiles. In January 2010, West Ham were found guilty of the charges of failure to control their fans at Upton Park and fined £115,000. Millwall's racism charge, allegedly for the racial abuse of Hammers striker Carlton Cole, was dropped and Millwall got away without a charge to their name. 54 West Ham supporters were banned for life from Upton Park after Operation Balconi, an operation specifically made to target the troublemakers, was set up.

As the dust settled in East London, calls for future games between the pair to be played closed doors were sounded out, with former Hammers manager Harry Redknapp going one further, saying any cup draw that draws the two together would need to be re-drawn completely, with league games taking place behind closed doors. That'd go down well.

The Hammers failed to win another game until November. Although they eventually secured Premier League survival, Zola paid with his job, with Portsmouth manager Avram Grant being appointed by new West Ham owners David Gold and David Sullivan. On the other side of the divide, Millwall finally ended their play-off hoodoo. Missing out on automatic promotion by a point, the Lions overcame Huddersfield Town in the play-off semi-finals, beating the Terriers by two goals to nil at The Den in a professional performance, following a bore draw up north. In front of 73,180 spectators at the new Wembley, Paul Robinson poked home a first half winner against Swindon Town, banishing Millwall's play-off heartbreak from 360 days earlier, after Scunthorpe United came from behind to pip Millwall to the Championship.

The Lions made a good impression back in the second tier of England, finish eighth in their first season back in the Championship. As for West Ham, two decent cup runs was as good as it got. The Hammers travelled up north to

Wigan Athletic on the 37th game of the season, knowing that only a win would secure their Premier League status for another week. January signing Demba Ba scored two first half goals to send West Ham into the half-time break 2-0 up. Charles N'Zogbia pulled a goal back for Wigan, before Conor Sammon levelled the scores with a smart finish past Rob Green on 68 minutes. Three minutes later, a faint humming could be heard above the DW Stadium. A light aircraft was spotted in the overcast skies above Wigan Athletic's home, trailing a banner that read "Avram Grant – Millwall Legend". The good-humoured banner was funded by members of Millwall's House of Fun forum, with planning starting a whole seven days before West Ham's trip to Wigan, after a 1-1 draw at home to Blackburn Rovers 24 hours previously left the Hammers needing a miracle to survive. A second N'Zogbia goal deep into added time confirmed West Ham's relegation, leaving the Hammers red-faced on and off the pitch.

on 8th may around 6pm, potbelliedgladiator started a thread "if i was a rich man" and said he'd hire a plane and banner to fly over wigan. A few hours and a few posts later, around 9pm, another member, Griffiths,suggested the idea of 100 or clubbing together £5 each.

The beginning of the write-up on House of Fun's website regarding their plane stunt.

In the aftermath of the Hammers' relegation to the second tier for the first time since 2003, rumours began circulating that away fans would be banned from both fixtures between the two in the 2011-12 season, a rumour the Metropolitan Police quickly put to bed. West Ham's relegation back to the Championship meant that, much like during their spell in their stint in the Championship during the mid-2000s, rivalries were renewed. On the opening weekend of the 2011-12 season, Cardiff City travelled down to East London, with a ticket allocation of only 1,250. The game was declared a 'bubble match', meaning Cardiff fans were only permitted to travel to Upton Park via official club coaches, picking up their match tickets at South Mimms services. Cardiff, however, had the last laugh on the rainy

August afternoon, picking the three points, courtesy of a 91st minute winner from Kenny Miller.

A month and ten days later, though, was the tie everybody had been anticipating, ever since the Championship fixtures were released in mid-June. Armed with tear gas, it was clear the police were much more prepared than two years prior; newly appointed West Ham manager Sam Allardyce would later hail the police's handling of the game as "a fantastic piece of organisation" after a London-wide policing operation was implemented. The same could not be said for Millwall's defence in the opening ten seconds of the tie. A "WELCOME TO BANDIT COUNTRY" banner hung proudly from the Dockers Stand greeted the teams as they exited the tunnel into a cacophony of noise. After losing the ball straight from kick-off, Millwall were almost left with egg on their face after Henri Lansbury, starting just his second game for the club after his loan move from Arsenal, fired just wide from 40 yards, missing an open goal with David Forde, who was on West Ham's books in the early 2000s, caught napping, more focused on attending to a drink of water, rather than starting the game in his goal. In a cagey tie, West

Ham came closest in the first half to open the scoring, with Lansbury seeing his shot cleared off the line by the head of Millwall captain Paul Robinson, who was finally making his debut in the derby after being ruled out of the previous five derbies between the two due to injuries and suspension. With just under a quarter of an hour left to play, the Hammers' new boy David Bentley, on loan from Tottenham, had the chance to make himself an instant hero, however, the midfielder couldn't convert a golden opportunity from seven yards out after Forde parried a shot from Julien Faubert. No major incidents were reported on a sunny afternoon in Bermondsey – a stark contrast from the scenes that marred 2009's League Cup clash between the pair.

Millwall's form took a considerable nosedive in the weeks following the game, with the Lions conceding eleven goals in their next four outings, including a 5-0 League Cup capitulation at home to Wolverhampton Wanderers. By the festive period, Millwall were hovering precariously above the relegation zone, whilst West Ham were eyeing an immediate return to the Premier League, sitting in the automatic promotion places on Christmas Day.

A month before the return fixture between the two, Millwall were drawn away to League Two side Dagenham & Redbridge in the third round of the FA Cup. With Dagenham being a hotbed of West Ham support, the propensity for violence was always lurking. Prior to the 0-0 draw at Victoria Road, a number of scuffles broke out close to the ground and at The Eastbrook pub, with the tie being chosen by several 'old school' names due to the location, the big crossover of fanbases between Dagenham and West Ham and the belief that there would be a lower police presence. The Met Police had clearly done their research, however, and a large police presence greeted the two sides. A number of West Ham and Millwall fans saw themselves up in court the following year for their roles organising the violence.

Although not a lot would suspect it at the time, February 2012's meeting would transpire to be the last derby between the two at Upton Park. The Summer Olympics were due to be contested in Stratford a few months later, over two miles away from Upton Park. West Ham were strong favourites to take up tenancy of the Olympic Stadium, although bids and legal processes between West Ham, Tottenham Hotspur and Leyton Orient meant West Ham wouldn't be officially confirmed as tenants of the site for some time yet.

Keen to avoid the scenes witness last time the two met at Upton Park, another London-wide operation was put into place by the police, with a complete alcohol ban in the stadium and all pubs and off-licenses around the ground put into place. In a further effort to prevent any unsavoury scenes, the 1,426 travelling Millwall supporters were placed in the upper tier of the Trevor Brooking Stand, with the lower tier completely empty – similar to the set-up Millwall frequently use when away fans visit The Den. Players from both sides were also warned to celebrate with an element of restraint by the police. Stanislas' celebrations clearly sticking in the mind from over two years ago.

Back on the pitch, West Ham came into the derby off the back of a 5-1 loss against Ipswich Town four days prior, the first time the Hammers had lost by four goals in the second tier of English football in 55 years. Millwall, on the other hand, also came into the game following a defeat, losing 2-0 at home to Watford. They did, however, overcome Dagenham in their FA Cup replay, with a young Harry Kane, on loan in South London, netting twice in a 5-0 win back at The Den.

Typically, the tie started off in a fiery fashion, with Hammers captain Kevin Nolan being given his marching orders after just eight minutes after contesting a loose ball with both feet off the ground, with Millwall defender Jack Smith needing treatment as a result of the challenge.

On the stroke of half-time, Hammers forward Carlton Cole outmuscled Darren Ward to a second ball, guiding a looping header past Forde to send West Ham into the break a goal to the good. Twenty minutes into the second period, Liam Trotter, Millwall's captain for the day, struck a cultured finish past the outstretched palm of Rob Green, a volley from just inside the 18-yard area that could grace any level of the game. The away end's delight would be short lived. Just three minutes later, the home side would find themselves back in the lead, albeit in controversial circumstances. Chasing a long ball forward, Faubert completely cleaned out Forde, allowing Winston Reid to volley home from just outside the box.

Millwall's protests were fruitless and the goal stood, with Reid's goal, which turned out to be the winner, being the first step in his securing cult hero status. Goals away at Tottenham and scoring the final ever goal at Upton Park, a winner against Manchester United in May 2016, would cement his status amongst the West Ham fanbase. Seeing no further goals, West Ham secured their first league win against their bitter rivals in 21 years. With no fireworks to speak of, apart from a single one let off from the away end during West Ham's final recital of I'm Forever Blowing Bubbles at full-time, the game passed off largely without disorder or incident, with only two arrests, a massive improvement from two years earlier.

Although the win kept West Ham on top of the table, four points clear of nearest challengers Southampton, a run of five consecutive draws during March saw the Hammers drop down to third. A home loss against fellow promotion chasers Reading effectively consigned West Ham to their third play-off campaign in ten years. After dispatching old foes Cardiff with ease, winning 5-0 over two legs, West Ham and their support made the trip across town to Wembley for the first time in 31 years, playing at the new Wembley for the first time. A hard fought 2-1 victory against Blackpool saw West Ham return to the Premier League after a year away in the wilderness. Millwall eventually pulled themselves out of any relegation dog fight, completing the season with five wins and two draws, finishing the season in 16th place, 17 points off the relegation zone.

With West Ham back in the top flight of English football, West Ham's bid to be the tenants of the Olympic Stadium strengthened. On 22 May 2013, West Ham were officially confirmed as the tenants of the stadium on a 99-year lease. The deal came after the previous decision, also selecting West Ham as the tenants of the stadium, collapsed two years prior due to legal issues.

Later that spring, Millwall confirmed the appointment of former Northern Irish international manager Steve Lomas as manager. Lomas had enjoyed a successive stint at Scottish club St Johnstone, guiding the club to the Europa League after an impressive third place finish in the Scottish Premier League. Lomas would've been a shrewd, clever appointment if not for one major sticking point. He had played for West Ham. Not only that, he had played for West Ham for eight years, captained the club, made 227 appearances and managed their reserves. Lomas' appointment was met with discontent at The Den and a poor start at the club did nothing to boost his popularity, finally winning his first league game at the club at the seventh attempt. Lomas was eventually sacked on Boxing Day after a 4-0 loss away to Watford. In 2019, Lomas conceded that his spell at Millwall was hindered by his extensive West Ham links.

In early November 2014, the pair were drawn to face each other once again, albeit in the differing climates of the Under-21 Premier League Cup. Drawn at home, in normal circumstances, West Ham would've hosted the tie at the Boleyn Ground, however were forced to relocate the tie to their Rush Green Stadium training site under police advice, with no spectators permitted. The decision to play the tie behind closed doors may have been influenced by a section of the 6,000 or so attending a Celtic v Rangers under-17 cup final north of the border the previous year letting off a number of flares, smoke bombs and breaking seats, the latter of which littered the perimeter of the pitch. Later that month, the two faced each other, with the only form of atmosphere coming from the faint sound of mainline trains zooming towards the City on the railway line 600 metres away. Goalless after 90 minutes, bright prospect Fred Onyedinma opened the scoring for Millwall in extra time, with 112 minutes on the clock, before Jaanai Gordon equalised with a header just two minutes later, sending the contest to a penalty shoot-out. The Hammers prevailed in the shoot-out 8-7, with substitute Dylan Casey missing Millwall's decisive spot kick. Managed by Millwall legend Neil Harris, who would later manage the Lions permanently from 2015 to 2019, Millwall's team featured two players, Jack Powell and Josh Siafa, who previously plied their trade in West Ham's development squad.

2016 rolled around with West Ham becoming the latest club to move to a more sanitised footballing arena in the Olympic Stadium, since renamed to the London Stadium, after the Hammers took up tenancy of the ground. West Ham's move from their previous home of 112 years edged the two rivals slightly closer geographically. As West Ham were getting acclimatised to their new surroundings, Lewisham Council purchased land around The Den in a compulsory purchase order in September 2016. Rumours swirled of Millwall having to once again relocate, with the club conceding the North Kent coast was an opinion. Eventually, the compulsory purchase order of the land was abandoned in the new year. Before that though, in December 2016, the two were drawn to play each other in the third round of the FA Cup. No extra policing was needed, however, due to the two only being paired together in a rehearsal. West Ham were eventually drawn at home to Manchester City, losing 5-0 in the first FA Cup tie at their shiny, new stadium. Millwall fared much better in the competition, beating Premier League holders Leicester City on the way to the quarter-finals, before exiting the competition at the hands of Tottenham.

Despite all the hatred and hostility this rivalry clearly emanates, there's definitely a more subtle and lighter side of the rivalry that goes under the radar. In February 2017, Southend defender Anton Ferdinand, who made over 150 appearances for West Ham, ran the risk of inciting a riot after saluting the away end at The Den with a 'Hammers' gesture after a 1-0 loss in a key League One clash. Although there's no doubt some choice language would've been directed towards Ferdinand, that was as far as it went. Millwall's efforts at cleaning up their image, starting in the mid-'70s with Gordon Jago, was finally rewarded later in 2017, with the club winning the Football League Family Club of the Year award. In December 2017, West Ham and Millwall were once again paired in the FA Cup third round draw rehearsal. The pair were given two decidedly more boring ties, in Shrewsbury Town and Barnsley respectively. The cup near misses were to continue into 2019. AFC Wimbledon were drawn to play Millwall in the fifth round of the FA Cup. You'll never guess who Wimbledon beat in the previous round. An early Murray Wallace goal was enough for the Lions to progress in the quarter-finals for the second time in three years, reigniting the Lions of the South spirit 119 years on from their famous cup exploits.

The rivalry between Millwall and West Ham is multi-faceted and shrouded in as much myth as it is reality. At times, the derby has resembled something more out of *Saving Private Ryan*, especially at Harry Cripps' testimonial in '72. But, despite all the bad press the two can attract when they meet, the two fanbases can come together to work for something more important than football. In 2019, a number of Millwall fans put their allegiances to one side to support Isla Caton, a young West Ham supporter who was diagnosed with neuroblastoma – a rare type of cancer that affects young children, raising thousands of pounds in the process. At the end of the day, the clubs can't stand each other, but can't live without each other.

Results

14 December 1895: Millwall Athletic Reserves 6-0 Thames Ironworks

Athletic Grounds; friendly

24 April 1896: Thames Ironworks 1-1 Millwall Athletic Reserves

Hermit Road; friendly

23 September 1897: Thames Ironworks 0-2 Millwall Athletic

Memorial Grounds; friendly

9 December 1899: Thames Ironworks 1-2 Millwall Athletic

Memorial Grounds; FA Cup fifth qualifying round

23 December 1899: Thames Ironworks 0-2 Millwall Athletic (abandoned

due to fog after 71 minutes)

Memorial Grounds; Southern League Division One

28 April 1900: Millwall Athletic 0-1 Thames Ironworks

Athletic Grounds; Southern League Division One

8 September 1900: Millwall Athletic 3-1 West Ham United

Athletic Grounds; Southern League

10 November 1900: Millwall Athletic 0-0 West Ham United

Athletic Grounds; friendly

22 December 1900: West Ham United 0-2 Millwall Athletic (abandoned

due to fog after 70 minutes)

Memorial Grounds; Southern League

26 December 1900: Millwall Athletic 6-0 West Ham United

North Greenwich; friendly

21 March 1901: West Ham United 1-0 Millwall Athletic (re-arranged match from 22 December 1900)

Memorial Grounds; Southern League

17 April 1901: Millwall Athletic 0-0 West Ham United

Athletic Grounds; friendly

9 September 1901: West Ham United 4-0 Millwall Athletic

Memorial Grounds; London League

26 October 1901: West Ham United 0-2 Millwall Athletic

Memorial Grounds; Southern League

26 December 1901: Millwall Athletic 1-5 West Ham United

North Greenwich; London League

8 February 1902: Millwall Athletic 1-1 West Ham United

North Greenwich; Southern League

5 April 1902: West Ham United 0-1 Millwall Athletic

Memorial Grounds; Western League Division One

9 April 1902: West Ham United 2-1 Millwall Athletic

Memorial Grounds; Southern Professional Charity Cup

26 April 1902: Millwall Athletic 1-0 West Ham United

North Greenwich; Western League Division One

6 October 1902: Millwall Athletic 1-0 West Ham United (abandoned due to fog after 60 minutes)

North Greenwich; Western League

6 October 1902: Millwall Athletic 1-2 West Ham United (hour long friendly after fog cleared)

North Greenwich; friendly

8 November 1902: West Ham United 0-3 Millwall Athletic

Memorial Grounds; Southern League

24 November 1902: Millwall Athletic 2-1 West Ham United

North Greenwich; Western League

29 November 1902: Millwall Athletic 2-2 West Ham United

North Greenwich; London League

5 January 1903: West Ham United 2-2 Millwall Athletic

Memorial Grounds; London League

9 March 1903: West Ham United 2-2 Millwall Athletic

Memorial Grounds; Western League

2 April 1903: West Ham United 1-7 Millwall Athletic

Memorial Grounds; Southern Charity Cup

25 April 1903: Millwall Athletic 2-1 West Ham United

North Greenwich; Southern League

5 September 1903: Millwall Athletic 2-4 West Ham United

North Greenwich; Southern League

5 October 1903: West Ham United 0-3 Millwall Athletic

Memorial Grounds; London League

2 January 1904: West Ham United 0-1 Millwall Athletic

Memorial Grounds; Southern League

29 February 1904: Millwall Athletic 4-0 West Ham United

North Greenwich; London League

1 September 1904: West Ham United 3-0 Millwall Athletic

Boleyn Ground; Southern League

17 September 1904: Millwall Athletic 1-1 West Ham United

North Greenwich; Southern League

20 March 1905: West Ham United 4-3 Millwall Athletic

Boleyn Ground; Western League

24 April 1905: Millwall Athletic 4-0 West Ham United

North Greenwich; Western League

29 April 1905: West Ham United 1-2 Millwall Athletic

Boleyn Ground; friendly

9 September 1905: Millwall Athletic 1-0 West Ham United

North Greenwich; Southern League

25 December 1905: Millwall Athletic 0-0 West Ham United

North Greenwich; Western League

6 January 1906: West Ham United 1-0 Millwall Athletic

Boleyn Ground; Southern League

16 April 1906: West Ham United 0-1 Millwall Athletic

Boleyn Ground; Western League

17 September 1906: West Ham United 1-0 Millwall Athletic

Boleyn Ground; Western League

13 October 1906: Millwall Athletic 1-1 West Ham United

North Greenwich; Southern League

19 November 1906: Millwall Athletic 0-3 West Ham United

North Greenwich; Western League

16 February 1907: West Ham United 0-1 Millwall Athletic

Boleyn Ground; Southern League

9 September 1907: Millwall Athletic 3-0 West Ham United

North Greenwich; Western League

16 September 1907: West Ham United 1-1 Millwall Athletic

Boleyn Ground; Western League

26 October 1907: Millwall Athletic 1-0 West Ham United

North Greenwich; Southern League

22 February 1908: West Ham United 0-2 Millwall Athletic

Boleyn Ground; Southern League

7 September 1908: West Ham United 0-2 Millwall Athletic

Boleyn Ground; Western League Division One

14 September 1908: Millwall Athletic 3-1 West Ham United

North Greenwich; Western League Division One

7 November 1908: West Ham United 1-0 Millwall Athletic

Boleyn Ground; Southern League

13 March 1909: Millwall Athletic 3-0 West Ham United

North Greenwich; Southern League

26 April 1909: West Ham United 5-1 Millwall Athletic

Boleyn Ground; London PFA Charity Fund

20 September 1909: West Ham United 1-0 Millwall Athletic

Boleyn Ground; London Challenge Cup first round

13 November 1909: Millwall Athletic 0-0 West Ham United

North Greenwich; Southern League

26 March 1910: West Ham United 1-2 Millwall Athletic

Boleyn Ground; Southern League

24 September 1910: Millwall 0-2 West Ham United

North Greenwich; Southern League

28 January 1911: West Ham United 2-2 Millwall

Boleyn Ground; Southern League

18 April 1911: Millwall 3-2 West Ham United

The Den; friendly

4 November 1911: West Ham United 2-1 Millwall

Boleyn Ground; Southern League

9 March 1912: Millwall 5-1 West Ham United

The Den; Southern League

22 September 1912: West Ham United 6-2 Millwall

Boleyn Ground; London Challenge Cup first round

30 November 1912: West Ham United 1-1 Millwall

Boleyn Ground; Southern League

5 April 1913: Millwall 1-3 West Ham United

The Den; Southern League

1 September 1913: Millwall 1-1 West Ham United

The Den; Southern League

22 September 1913: West Ham United 0-1 Millwall

Boleyn Ground; London Challenge Cup first round

14 April 1914: West Ham United 3-2 Millwall

Boleyn Ground; Southern League

17 October 1914: Millwall 2-1 West Ham United

The Den; Southern League

9 November 1914: West Ham United 0-1 Millwall

Boleyn Ground; London Challenge Cup semi-final

20 February 1915: West Ham United 1-1 Millwall

Boleyn Ground; Southern League

30 October 1915: West Ham United 2-1 Millwall

Boleyn Ground; London Combination (principle)

15 January 1916: Millwall 1-0 West Ham United

The Den; London Combination (principle)

12 February 1916: Millwall 1-0 West Ham United

The Den; London Combination (supplementary)

18 March 1916: West Ham United 2-1 Millwall

Boleyn Ground; London Combination (supplementary)

23 September 1916: Millwall 2-4 West Ham United

The Den; London Combination

10 April 1917: West Ham United 0-2 Millwall

Boleyn Ground; London Combination

22 September 1917: Millwall 2-3 West Ham United

The Den; London Combination

17 November 1917: West Ham United 0-0 Millwall

Boleyn Ground; London Combination

12 January 1918: Millwall 0-1 West Ham United

The Den; London Combination

9 March 1918: West Ham United 2-0 Millwall

Boleyn Ground; London Combination

25 December 1918: Millwall 0-2 West Ham United

The Den; London Combination

26 December 1918: West Ham United 2-0 Millwall

Boleyn Ground; London Combination

15 February 1919: Millwall 2-2 West Ham United

The Den; London Combination

12 April 1919: West Ham United 3-2 Millwall

Boleyn Ground; London Combination

17 May 1919: Millwall 4-0 West Ham United

The Den; friendly

20 October 1919: Millwall 3-4 West Ham United (3-3 after 90 minutes;

match abandoned after 105 minutes)

The Den; London PFA Charity Fund

14 April 1920: Millwall 1-3 West Ham United (re-arranged match from

October 1919)

The Den; London PFA Charity Fund

15 November 1920: Millwall 0-1 West Ham United

The Den; London PFA Charity Fund

8 October 1923: Millwall 2-0 West Ham United

The Den; London PFA Charity Cup final

5 November 1923: Millwall 2-1 West Ham United

The Den; London Challenge Cup second round

13 October 1924: West Ham United 3-1 Millwall

Boleyn Ground; London PFA Charity Cup

25 October 1926: West Ham United 5-2 Millwall (match abandoned)

Boleyn Ground; London PFA Charity Cup

22 November 1926: West Ham United 1-1 Millwall (re-arranged match

from October 1926; West Ham awarded win by coin toss)

Boleyn Ground; London PFA Charity Cup

10 October 1927: West Ham United 1-5 Millwall

Boleyn Ground; London PFA Charity Cup final

8 October 1928: West Ham United 5-1 Millwall

Boleyn Ground; London PFA Charity Cup final

18 November 1929: Millwall 2-1 West Ham United (abandoned due to fog

on 71 minutes)

The Den; London Challenge Cup third round

25 November 1929: Millwall 2-4 West Ham United (re-arranged London

Challenge Cup match)

The Den; London Challenge Cup

15 February 1930: West Ham United 4-1 Millwall

Boleyn Ground; FA Cup fifth round

17 September 1932: West Ham United 3-0 Millwall

Boleyn Ground; Second Division

30 January 1933: Millwall 1-0 West Ham United

The Den; Second Division

21 October 1933: Millwall 2-2 West Ham United

The Den; Second Division

3 March 1934: West Ham United 1-1 Millwall

Boleyn Ground; Second Division

27 December 1938: West Ham United 0-0 Millwall

Boleyn Ground; Second Division

27 March 1938: Millwall 0-2 West Ham United

The Den; Second Division

30 September 1939: West Ham United 2-1 Millwall

Boleyn Ground; friendly

11 November 1939: Millwall 2-2 West Ham United

The Den; Football League South A

30 December 1939: West Ham United 6-2 Millwall

Boleyn Ground; Football League South A

2 March 1940: Millwall 4-0 West Ham United

The Den; Football League South C

3 June 1940: West Ham United 1-2 Millwall

Craven Cottage; Football League South C

12 October 1940: West Ham United 3-2 Millwall

Boleyn Ground; Football League South

19 October 1940: Millwall 2-2 West Ham United

The Den; Football League South

4 January 1941: Millwall 1-2 West Ham United

The Den; London War Cup B Division

11 January 1941: West Ham United 2-1 Millwall

Boleyn Ground; London War Cup B Division

2 June 1941: West Ham United 0-3 Millwall

Boleyn Ground; Football League South

11 October 1941: West Ham United 4-2 Millwall

Boleyn Ground; London War League

17 February 1942: Millwall 1-3 West Ham United

The Den; London War League

23 May 1942: West Ham United 6-2 Millwall
Boleyn Ground; friendly

14 November 1942: West Ham United 7-5 Millwall
Boleyn Ground; Football League South

20 February 1943: Millwall 3-3 West Ham United
The Den; Football League South

13 November 1943: West Ham United 3-0 Millwall
Boleyn Ground; Football League South

29 April 1944: Millwall 1-3 West Ham United
The Den; Football League South

28 October 1944: Millwall 0-3 West Ham United
The Den; Football League South

24 March 1945: West Ham United 3-1 Millwall
Boleyn Ground; Football League South

20 October 1945: Millwall 0-0 West Ham United
The Den; Football League South

27 October 1945: West Ham United 3-1 Millwall
Boleyn Ground; Football League South

21 September 1946: West Ham United 3-1 Millwall
Boleyn Ground; Second Division

25 January 1947: Millwall 0-0 West Ham United
The Den; Second Division

25 August 1947: West Ham United 1-1 Millwall
Boleyn Ground; Second Division

1 September 1947: Millwall 1-1 West Ham United
The Den; Second Division

29 February 1949: West Ham United 1-1 Millwall
Boleyn Ground; friendly

31 October 1955: Millwall 2-4 West Ham United

The Den; friendly

13 October 1959: West Ham United 3-1 Millwall

Boleyn Ground; Southern Floodlit Cup first round

4 May 1972: Millwall 3-5 West Ham United

The Den; friendly (Harry Cripps testimonial)

3 December 1974: Millwall 3-4 West Ham United

The Den; friendly (Billy Neil testimonial)

7 October 1978: West Ham United 3-0 Millwall

Boleyn Ground; Second Division

14 May 1979: Millwall 2-1 West Ham United

The Den; Second Division

10 November 1987: West Ham United 1-2 Millwall

Boleyn Ground; Full Members' Cup

3 December 1988: Millwall 0-1 West Ham United

The Den; First Division

22 April 1989: West Ham United 3-0 Millwall

Boleyn Ground; First Division

10 November 1990: Millwall 1-1 West Ham United

The Den; Second Division

24 February 1991: West Ham United 3-1 Millwall

Boleyn Ground; Second Division

15 November 1992: Millwall 2-1 West Ham United

The Den; First Division

28 March 1993: West Ham United 2-2 Millwall

Boleyn Ground; First Division

28 September 2003: West Ham United 1-1 Millwall

Boleyn Ground; First Division

21 March 2004: Millwall 4-1 West Ham United

The New Den; First Division

21 November 2004: Millwall 1-0 West Ham United

The New Den; Championship

16 April 2005: West Ham United 1-1 Millwall

Boleyn Ground; Championship

25 August 2009: West Ham United 3-1 Millwall (1-1 after 90 minutes)

Boleyn Ground; League Cup second round

17 September 2011: Millwall 0-0 West Ham United

The New Den; Championship

4 February 2012: West Ham United 2-1 Millwall

Boleyn Ground; Championship

References

East Ham Echo, 1906. Football. p.1.

Evening Standard, 1899. Football notes. p. 10.

Evening Standard, 2003. West Ham v Millwall (Sunday, 12 noon). p. 256.

Evening Standard, 2009. Our last result. p. 55.

Korr, C., 1978. West Ham United Football Club and the Beginnings of Professional Football in East London, 1895-1914. *Journal of Contemporary History*, 13(2), pp.211-232.

Millwall matchday programme, 1974. Millwall F.C. p. 2.

The Guardian, 1930. Football. p. 3.

The Guardian, 1965. Shameful behaviour at two World Cup grounds. p. 11.

The Guardian, 1997. Bonzo bounces back. p. 58.

The Guardian, 1998. Millwall end their ties with Bonds. p. 68.

Stratford Express, 1906. Football. p.1.

Stratford Express, 1966. World Cup special. p.1

9 781913 454562

Printed by BoD™in Norderstedt, Germany